EXODUS devotional

~ VOLUME ONE ~

~ Laying Down Your Idols ~

OTHER BOOKS BY GWEN SHAMBLIN

RISE ABOVE

THE WEIGH DOWN† DIET

EXODUS devotional

~ VOLUME ONE ~

~ Laying Down Your Idols ~

GWEN SHAMBLIN

Published in Franklin, Tennessee, by The Weigh Down Workshop, Inc.

ISBN 1-892729-77-6

INTRODUCTION

We are all travelers on a short journey. On this journey, we find ourselves surrounded by a maze of opportunities with countless choices. The consequences of continually making the wrong choices have led to many a troubling day for most of us. Oh, to wake up and have continual dependence and concentration on God the Father and Jesus Christ the Son!

I pray that the thoughts in this book will help you develop a deeper relationship with God. The Apostle Paul told others to imitate him as he imitated Jesus Christ. He was not being conceited or arrogant; rather, he was desperate to help bring peace into the lives of many seekers. It is, after all, a seeking process—a continual seeking process. I hope that this book will help you understand how I think about the Father and how I love Him with all my heart. I believe that the perspective I have about the heart of the heavenly Father has made all the difference in making the choices that I have made over the last few decades.

The God of the universe is trying to get through to us. He is asking us to seek out His personality, His job descriptions, and His governing decisions. He is asking us to love, respect, and trust all the decisions He makes about life and death, love and hate, light and darkness, and yesterday and tomorrow. I cannot express to you how much I love Him and how I love every decision He makes—from the ingenious color of the grass (it could have been purple or brown, but I love green) to the natural process of death to the physical body that brings us home to a new life with Him.

True happiness can be found in an intelligent perspective of what is going on. In John 15:15, Jesus said, "I no longer call you servants, because a servant does not know his master's business. Instead, I have called you friends, for everything that I learned from my Father I have made known to you." The more you learn about the mind of God and experience His plan for your life, the more you can live like a child—full of happiness and peace with excited anticipation about the mystery of each coming day instead of living each day in worry and fear!

I hope that the pages of this book will help you understand the wonderful but dangerous jealousy of the Father. We are not to play around with the love of the Father! We should respect and fearfully adore this opportunity to make the right choice to fall in love with Him. It is a daily choice until the heart is deeply embedded in pure love for the Father.

And I hope that the scriptures, thoughts, and observations you are about to read will help you develop this mind-set as you learn about His love for you and as you take your personal journey, reflecting on where He has directed your heart and mind during each new lesson.

With love,

EXODUS BASICS

JESUS IS THE CORNERSTONE

Consequently, you are no longer foreigners and aliens, but fellow citizens with God's people and members of God's household, built on the foundation of the apostles and prophets, with Christ Jesus himself as the chief cornerstone.

—*Ephesians 2:19–20*

God has brought you here to join the mighty Exodus of people who are moving away from the slavery of food, dieting, bulimia, anorexia, and many other strongholds. The miserable state of slavery to food and diets is similar to the bondage the children of God felt when they were enslaved centuries ago to the Egyptian pharaohs. The book of Exodus tells us how God's children, once subjugated to Pharaoh, were forced into slave labor to build huge Egyptian structures, such as the pyramids. Those towering icons are representations of the strength and the soul that the Israelites invested in Egypt. May we all reinvest our souls in preparing our hearts to be used to build the church of God with Jesus Christ as the cornerstone.

Start your new year by reviewing God's salvation. Review the basics of how God has saved us from having to love this earth and how we get to love Him. What a salvation! And take a fresh look at the true Jesus Christ who is portrayed in the scriptures. He showed us by His life that He lived daily to do the will of God.

How I Can Do God's Will Today

_____
_____
_____
_____
_____
_____
_____
_____
_____
_____
_____
_____
_____
_____
_____
_____
_____
_____
_____
_____
_____
_____
_____
_____
_____
_____
_____

January 2

GOD CAN DELIVER YOU

During the night Pharaoh summoned Moses and Aaron and said, "Up! Leave my people, you and the Israelites! Go, worship the LORD as you have requested. Take your flocks and herds, as you have said, and go. And also bless me."

—Exodus 12:31–32

The Exodus story has meaning for us today. This foundational story is used throughout the Old Testament and the New Testament and is used for warnings and instruction by Jesus, Stephen, and the Apostle Paul. To start with, I believe that Egypt is symbolic of this earth and anything on earth with which we can fall in love. The symbolism is that we can worship anything and let it control us—cigarettes, alcohol, money, food, or the praise of men. You are bowing down to any habit that you want to quit, but that now controls you. What is on your mind and what you find yourself worrying about is your god. But just as God delivered the Israelites from the slavery of Pharaoh, He can deliver you today. Make Him your destiny, make Him your one true God, and give Him all the glory. And He will take you away from earthly things and let you worship Him instead. God can deliver you if you will start today letting Him be your God. You are not the god of your body. You are not the god of indulgence. Your Creator is. Submit to THE GOD and your Exodus will begin today!

How I Can Do God's Will Today

January 4

THE KEY TO A HIGHER LOVE

But the Israelites went through the sea on dry ground, with a wall of water on their right and on their left. That day the LORD saved Israel from the hands of the Egyptians, and Israel saw the Egyptians lying dead on the shore. And when the Israelites saw the great power the LORD displayed against the Egyptians, the people feared the LORD and put their trust in him and in Moses his servant.

—Exodus 14:29-31

We have all started off in Egypt. In other words, we have all given our devotion to something on this earth, becoming slaves to the things we love. Since we are slaves to what we love, it will take an even *stronger love* to remove us. God showed the Israelites His passionate, jealous love, and He let them know that He was not going to sit still and let Egypt enslave them. Egypt was exposed for what it was—worthless—and God showed His love and power in an incredible display of devastating plagues and powerful deliverance. The children of God made the right choice and followed Him out of Egypt, into the desert, and finally to the Promised Land. There is no love that compares to the love of God! But remember, the key to the love of God is having a reverent fear of His Lordship and then trusting Him and His true servants.

How I Can Do God's Will Today

January 6

WHAT ARE YOUR IDOLS?

He said to me, "Son of man, have you seen what the elders of the house of Israel are doing in the darkness, each at the shrine of his own idol? They say, 'The LORD does not see us; the LORD has forsaken the land.'" Again, he said, "You will see them doing things that are even more detestable." Then he brought me to the entrance to the north gate of the house of the LORD, and I saw women sitting there, mourning for Tammuz [a false god]. He said to me, "Do you see this, son of man? You will see things that are even more detestable than this."

—Ezekiel 8:12–15

Many people have given their love to Egypt and its idols, yet they are not aware of what they are giving their devotion and energy to. There are several ways to find out if something is an idol in your life. The first is what we ask people to do in Weigh Down†: let the object, such as your extra food, be taken away. If you still long for it, you know that your heart has been given over to that idol. Something even more detestable to God—even more than finding out that you are bowing down to a false god—is seeing you mourning and pining over the idol. If you have tried to separate yourself from food or any stronghold and you are sad about it, your response really hurts God.

Another way to identify an idol is to examine what you think about all the time. What do you worry about? That is where your heart is. If you find that your heart is enslaved or mourning over an idol or many idols, pray to the Father to free you from your anguish. Never mourn over the food you have left behind, and strengthen your focus on God each time your heart feels troubled. One day you will realize that God has taken over as your heart's true desire, and you will feel light and free!

January 7

HOW I CAN DO GOD'S WILL TODAY

_____

_____

_____

_____

_____

_____

_____

_____

_____

_____

_____

_____

_____

_____

_____

_____

_____

_____

_____

_____

_____

_____

_____

_____

_____

_____

_____

January 8

ARE YOU HUNGRY
AND THIRSTY FOR GOD?

"Blessed are those who hunger and thirst for righteousness, for they will be filled."

—Matthew 5:6

God created food to fill our physical bodies, to nourish our muscles and cells, and to give us strength and health. But if you have been in Weigh Down[†] for any time at all, you have realized that mere food is not enough to truly fill our spirits and souls—in fact, it doesn't come close. That's because that is not the purpose for which food was created. All of us have an inner hunger and thirst for something, and it will not be satisfied by food, money, sexual lust, television, sports, shopping, or any other worldly pursuit. This is a hunger for God, and the only thing that will fill you up is obeying God and working in His kingdom. Jesus said, "My food is to do the will of the Father." You will soon learn that you are filled *in the doing.*

When you recognize this hunger for what it is and you satisfy it with seeking and obeying God and His Word and His guidance, you will be filled. This ultimate longing is a stronger hunger than any physical hunger, and the fulfillment of your purpose will satisfy you more than any food could ever satisfy physical hunger. You will be filled, happy, and satisfied for all eternity!

January 9

How I Can Do God's Will Today

_____

_____

_____

_____

_____

_____

_____

_____

_____

_____

_____

_____

_____

_____

_____

_____

_____

_____

_____

_____

_____

_____

_____

_____

_____

_____

_____

_____

January 10

THE LAW OF SIN

Those who live according to the sinful nature have their minds set on what that nature desires; but those who live in accordance with the Spirit have their minds set on what the Spirit desires. The mind of sinful man is death, but the mind controlled by the Spirit is life and peace; the sinful mind is hostile to God. It does not submit to God's law, nor can it do so. Those controlled by the sinful nature cannot please God.

—Romans 8:5–8

The law of sin (overindulgence of any kind, materialism, the love of power or praise, anger, greed, malice, etc.) is somewhat like the law of gravity. It is real, it is strong, it pulls you down, and it is a force that must be reckoned with. If you have never addressed this compelling force of gravity or compelling force of sin head-on, then you might have some bruises when you begin the process of overcoming. *Strongholds* are well named. You can ignore the law of gravity and come to an early death. In the same way, you can ignore this law of sin (the magnetic pull to the love of worldly things) and come to an early spiritual death. The way to rise above the magnetic pull of sin is to get your focus off earthly things and on to being happy to do everything God's way because, after all, He is GOD. Practice flying above the pull of all worldly things with a new focus and a new heart. Practice this today because persons controlled by their strongholds *cannot* please God.

January 11

HOW I CAN DO GOD'S WILL TODAY

_____
_____
_____
_____
_____
_____
_____
_____
_____
_____
_____
_____
_____
_____
_____
_____
_____
_____
_____
_____
_____
_____
_____
_____
_____
_____
_____
_____
_____
_____

January 12

TEMPTATIONS AND DESIRE EATING

When tempted, no one should say, "God is tempting me." For God cannot be tempted by evil, nor does he tempt anyone; but each one is tempted when, by his own evil desire, he is dragged away and enticed. Then, after desire has conceived, it gives birth to sin; and sin, when it is full-grown, gives birth to death.

—James 1:13–15

Once you begin to wait for true physiological hunger, you discover that there is another feeling of hunger. It is your own "I'm not hungry, but I want it anyway" attitude. We will call this "desire eating" or "head hunger." And it is really a deep desire to be your own god or boss. To help you understand this idea, imagine a headstrong two-year-old child, prone to temper tantrums, who sees a toy, desires it, beats his hands on the floor to speed up the service, then grabs the toy and holds it close with a tightened grip. The desire is very strong, and the temptation to give in is strong. But remember that this temptation does not come from God; it comes from your own evil desire. Remember, too, that this temptation will lead to sin, which will lead to death. Be aware of your temptations for what they are, and be strong when you stand up to them. Think of God's love for you, and run to Him when your temptations are strong, for He is the way of life. Be afraid of sin—this powerful force that leads to death when it is full grown. Fear wanting to play God when you know you are not the creator and god of your body!

HOW I CAN DO GOD'S WILL TODAY

_____

January 14

GIVING YOUR ALL TO GOD

One of the teachers of the law came and heard them debating. Noticing that Jesus had given them a good answer, he asked him, "Of all the commandments, which is the most important?"

—Mark 12:28

Jesus answered the question noted in the opening verse by saying that the most important thing is to love God with all of your heart, soul, mind, and strength. Although the journey starts in the mind with knowledge of God, having the knowledge alone is not enough. You could have the knowledge of God but not love Him at all. You must have a whole heart for God!

We fell in love with food by giving it our hearts, souls, minds, and strength, *which is included in the one behavior called obedience.* We obeyed the food. It called us from bed in the morning, and we used our strength to prepare it. We used our strength to force more of it down into the body than the body called for. We gave it our minds all day long by looking through recipe books and discussing the latest diets with our friends, asking, "What do you get to eat on your diet?" We lusted after the foods that were on the menu, and we gave our hearts to the ten o'clock binge. To transfer this love to God, we need to fully obey God with all of our minds, hearts, souls, and strength. This means that with every breath we take, we give thanks to the Creator who allows us to live. Every time we obey God in regard to food or *anything* He puts on our hearts to work on, we will fall more in love with Him. Just as Paul taught, we must turn to God and prove our repentance by our deeds, or in other words, our obedience (Acts 26:20). We must remember this every day of the year.

January 15

How I Can Do God's Will Today

January 16

THE CRUSH

But if from there you seek the LORD your God, you will find him if you look for him with all your heart and with all your soul.

—*Deuteronomy 4:29*

Your first question might be: "What *is* your heart?" Well, the best way to describe loving with your heart is to liken it to the love you have for another person. If you have ever had a crush on someone, then you know how this feels. Your emotions rise, and your pulse rate goes up. You know if that person enters the room, for your senses are alert to the voice and presence of the one you love. You think about your heart's love every spare moment. You dress for that person, and you seek out opportunities to be in his or her presence. You look forward to your times alone. Separation brings sadness.

You see, your heart is an emotional entity. It has passion and feeling and devotion. God made our hearts, and we all have 100 percent of a heart. However, some people have given pieces of their hearts to things in this world that drain the life out of them until they have no heart left and are burned out. Seek the Lord as if you had a crush on Him, and devote your total heart to Him. Fill your heart's need for passion and devotion by focusing on your loving Authority and His will, and you *will* find Him, and you will be able to say with the psalmist, "As the deer pants for streams of water, so my soul pants for you, O God" (Psalm 42:1).

HOW I CAN DO GOD'S WILL TODAY

January 18

FREE FROM SIN

What shall we say, then? Shall we go on sinning so that grace may increase? By no means! We died to sin; how can we live in it any longer? Or don't you know that all of us who were baptized into Christ Jesus were baptized into his death? We were therefore buried with him through baptism into death in order that, just as Christ was raised from the dead through the glory of the Father, we too may live a new life. If we have been united with him like this in his death, we will certainly also be united with him in his resurrection. For we know that our old self was crucified with him so that the body of sin might be done away with, that we should no longer be slaves to sin—because anyone who has died has been freed from sin.

—Romans 6:1–7

One of the strongest statements in the New Testament occurs when the Apostle Paul said that we cannot continue in sin so that grace may abound. "By no means!" is a strong statement. You cannot find an argument that will allow you to stay under grace in a blatantly sinning state. Grace will not abound if that is what you think. Obviously that was an issue for the early Christians, and Paul set them straight in the next few chapters of Romans. We should learn from this teaching, too, and realize that since we have died to sin through Jesus, we should *by no means* live in sin any longer.

Sin is simply loving yourself—or anything on this earth or in heaven above—more than God. Sin is simply thinking you're the boss of God and therefore you can ignore the Boss and make all your own decisions. Sin is simply the arrogance of thinking that you have a better way of doing things. Arrogance is unemployable. You must be like Jesus and humble yourself to the Great CEO or King. Sin involves making a *choice* between humility or pride. Choose to obey the Boss and please Him—not yourself—and you will be free from sin.

HOW I CAN DO GOD'S WILL TODAY

January 20

GOD IS BETTER THAN A BINGE

Taste and see that the LORD is good; blessed is the man who takes refuge in him.

—Psalm 34:8

In the past you may have loved the feeling of planning a binge and dreaming about food. You may have looked forward to the feeling of waiting to be alone so you could prepare, cook, and consume the food without the judgment of anybody. But I'm sure you have learned by now that food cannot satisfy . . . the world cannot satisfy. This is true if you go after the intoxicated feeling, the antidepressant feeling, the feeling of sexual lust, the tobacco feeling, the love-of-money feeling, or the love-of-the-praise-of-people feeling. After you binge on the world and its pleasures, you are empty, left in need again.

The good news is that you can relearn how to get the satisfied feeling from the Lord. When you feed your longing soul with God, His will, and His personality, and when you experiment with talking to Him, doing things His way, having your prayers answered, and trusting Him, then love for God will fill your heart, and the old empty feeling will leave permanently. You start to feel fulfilled—not so "hungry" anymore. You discover that running to God for everything—worries, questions, help, and enjoyment—is delightful and so much better than a binge. Taste and see today!

January 21

HOW I CAN DO GOD'S WILL TODAY

January 22

MAKING THE FOOD BEHAVE

Since you died with Christ to the basic principles of this world, why, as though you still belonged to it, do you submit to its rules: "Do not handle! Do not taste! Do not touch!"? These are all destined to perish with use, because they are based on human commands and teachings. Such regulations indeed have an appearance of wisdom, with their self-imposed worship, their false humility and their harsh treatment of the body, but they lack any value in restraining sensual indulgence.

—Colossians 2:20–23

Nothing is inherently wrong with food, alcohol, tobacco, credit cards, tranquilizers, and sexual desire. What is wrong is with the *heart*. Making food have less fat is not going to make our hearts less greedy for food in the evening hours. I'm sure we've all experienced that in the past while on one diet or another. Tearing up a credit card is not going to keep our hearts from materialism. Just ask anyone who has cut up her credit cards only to find other ways to keep shopping. Locking someone up in a detoxification center to make him stop abusing alcohol or drugs is not going to fix his heart. That is why so many people return to the center once, twice, or many times to repeat the treatment. We can't just change what is around us and expect that to make us behave correctly. Making our food behave by removing the calories, sugar, and fat will not make us desire to eat less—that can come only from the heart. You could change your environment all you want to and yet still secretly kiss food. Examine your heart. Where do you truly need to make changes?

January 23

How I Can Do God's Will Today

_____
_____
_____
_____
_____
_____
_____
_____
_____
_____
_____
_____
_____
_____
_____
_____
_____
_____
_____
_____
_____
_____
_____
_____
_____
_____
_____
_____
_____
_____

January 24

How to Fall in Love

I love the LORD, for he heard my voice; he heard my cry for mercy.
Because he turned his ear to me, I will call on him as long as I live.
—Psalm 116:1–2

We have talked a lot about choosing God. So, what are some more ways to fall in love with God? Think about it. How did you fall in love with food or other strongholds—cigarettes, alcohol, money, or pornography? What happened was that our hearts became enslaved to strongholds by *obeying* the strongholds. Look at food as an example. When the potato chips called our names from the pantry and said, "Hey, come eat me," we listened and obeyed. When we thought about a great steak dinner, we felt our emotions rise. Our pulse rate went up. Our senses were alert to the sounds and presence of popcorn popping, steak sizzling, corn boiling, and candy wrappers opening. We found ourselves dressing for eating occasions, preferring elastic outfits with no belts. We looked forward to times alone for a binge. We would do anything to get to food. Buying, preparing, and eating food were always pleasurable, while being separated from food brought sadness. Now transfer these actions to God. You will be greatly rewarded, for God will hear your cries, whereas the food cannot. God will turn His ear to you, whereas the food never can. Transfer your love by listening to, singing to, obeying, dressing for, anticipating, and longing for the Father. *Obeying* is the richest of all.

How I Can Do God's Will Today

_____
_____
_____
_____
_____
_____
_____
_____
_____
_____
_____
_____
_____
_____
_____
_____
_____
_____
_____
_____
_____
_____
_____
_____
_____
_____
_____
_____
_____

January 26

THE IDOLATRY OF GREED

Put to death, therefore, whatever belongs to your earthly nature: sexual immorality, impurity, lust, evil desires and greed, which is idolatry.

—Colossians 3:5

No immoral, impure or greedy person—such a man is an idolater—has any inheritance in the kingdom of Christ and of God.

—Ephesians 5:5

The Bible tells us that greed is idolatry, and as strange as that sounds, it is true. Let me explain. God is your Boss or Employer with a great business or kingdom. Life is a seventy-year job interview to see if you are employable in His kingdom. You cannot hire someone into your business who doesn't like the business plan, the boss's ideas, or the boss's decisions. If every day the boss says, "I want you to do this," and the employee arrogantly thinks he has a better idea and does it his own way, the employee is not fit to be a part of that business or kingdom. He will mess up the boss's plans and keep the business from growing. That employee is arrogant to think that *he* is a boss. He needs to start his own business and be humbled to find that he is not a boss or that he is not a god or a king.

If God has been telling you that a plate of food is what He has apportioned for you today, and you defy your Boss and say, "Oh, no. I'm eating three times plus a binge," then you are *arrogant*. You think you are a god, and you obviously do not like or submit to the Boss's ideas. Repent today and open your eyes to see how generous He is that we get to chew and swallow food every day.

January 27

How I Can Do God's Will Today

January 28

GOD'S GENEROUS REWARDS

And without faith it is impossible to please God, because anyone who comes to him must believe that he exists and that he rewards those who earnestly seek him.

—Hebrews 11:6

I will be giving tips all the way through this book to help you develop a heart that is passionate for this Father, CEO, Boss, Five-Star General, King, and Lord! Your first assignment is to take ten minutes away from food and give them to God. He doesn't need your ten minutes, so He gives you back twenty! Take that ten dollars away from the drive-through window and give it to God. Our God is *the* God and the *only* God. How do I know? He is the only One who will return the sacrifice I give Him, and He will send showers of blessings along with it. He doesn't need your money! However, food will *take* your ten dollars as well as your time and will ask only for more and more. God has it all, and He generously rewards hearts that love Him. If you run to Him for everything, you will be rewarded with great blessings or jewels.

Running to God for comfort and solutions makes sense. Do you need a counselor? He knows all truth, and His Word is a light unto your path. Do you need a friend? He is the God of all comfort. Are you low on money, need your roof fixed or your car repaired? God can provide. Are you looking for excitement? His kingdom is dynamic. God can do anything. He is the God who single-handedly defeated Pharaoh and his army and pulled the men, women, children, and livestock out of slavery to worship Him. He is the Warrior and Hero whom we can all fall in love with and follow away from this world that gives nothing back. He is the only real God. Have faith in Him, and follow Him out of Egypt, never to return.

January 21

HOW I CAN DO GOD'S WILL TODAY

January 30

GOD'S GRAVITATIONAL PULL

What causes fights and quarrels among you? Don't they come from your desires that battle within you? You want something but don't get it. You kill and covet, but you cannot have what you want. You quarrel and fight. You do not have, because you do not ask God. When you ask, you do not receive, because you ask with wrong motives, that you may spend what you get on your pleasures. You adulterous people, don't you know that friendship with the world is hatred toward God? Anyone who chooses to be a friend of the world becomes an enemy of God. ...That is why Scripture says: "God opposes the proud but gives grace to the humble." Submit yourselves, then, to God. Resist the devil, and he will flee from you. Come near to God and he will come near to you. Wash your hands, you sinners, and purify your hearts, you double-minded.

—James 4:1–8

God wants you to move away from the pull of the world and turn your path toward Him. As your heart draws nearer to God, you find that He draws nearer to you. His ways become increasingly attractive. You become unable to resist Him because His powerful, magnetic, wonderful force is so much stronger than the world's pull!

The sun, being much larger than the earth, has a stronger gravitational pull. We are not conscious of it because we are so far from the sun, but if a spaceship were launched out of earth's orbit, it would begin moving toward the sun's gravitational pull. The farther it traveled, the less earth's gravity would affect it and the greater the sun's attraction would become.

So how do *you* come near? *Remove all pride.* Admit that God has a better idea of how much food to eat. Accept the spouse God chose for you and don't even think you can lust after someone else. Let God decide your financial lot; be thankful for what He gives. God opposes the proud—those who believe they have a better idea of the indulgences they should have! Grace and salvation are for the humble.

January 31

HOW I CAN DO GOD'S WILL TODAY

— February 7

No One Can Serve Two Masters

"No servant can serve two masters. Either he will hate the one and love the other, or he will be devoted to the one and despise the other. You cannot serve both God and Money."

—Luke 16:13

You cannot drink the cup of the Lord and the cup of demons too; you cannot have a part in both the Lord's table and the table of demons.

—1 Corinthians 10:21

If you think that you can handle loving both food and God, you are fooling yourself, but you are not fooling God. No one can serve two masters. It cannot be done. Our hearts were created to be devoted to only one thing at a time. God is the One who created your heart this way, so you will never convince Him that you love Him when you are still a slave and servant to food or yourself. Instead, give your heart to the One who created it. Don't trust in yourself. Turn your heart against the excess food. Hate the food that your body doesn't need, and instead be fully devoted to God.

The fact that we cannot have two masters is very good news for all of us! Once you give your heart to God, you *cannot* give it to food (or to self or any other worldly idol) at the same time! Isn't it wonderful? When your master is the one true God, you will be repulsed by excess food or your own decisions. You will be approaching the Promised Land of having no desire to eat the second half of the plate of food! As it is stated in Galatians, if you live by the Spirit, you will not gratify the desires of your sinful nature. In other words, if God is your Employer, you will not listen to another boss or employer—and you will certainly know that *you* are not a good boss. Just look at the past decisions on how much to eat that you have made, and wake up and see that you are not good at being self-employed.

— February 2

HOW I CAN DO GOD'S WILL TODAY

February 3

THE GIFT OF LIFE

"Therefore, O house of Israel, I will judge you, each one according to his ways, declares the Sovereign LORD. Repent! Turn away from all your offenses; then sin will not be your downfall. Rid yourselves of all the offenses you have committed, and get a new heart and a new spirit. Why will you die, O house of Israel? For I take no pleasure in the death of anyone, declares the Sovereign LORD. Repent and live!"

—Ezekiel 18:30–32

It is a very nice thing that God has allowed you and me to have our lives. You know, there were many other egg cells and sperm cells for Him to pick from, but God let each of *us* be created and have a heart that beats and loves. It is also a very nice thing that He is giving us a chance to appreciate this life by loving Him first and then letting us enjoy the rest of the earth. With all this in mind, why would you consider loving His earthly creations and putting Him—the Great Creator—on the back burner? It doesn't make any sense. We should appreciate the wonderful gift of life He has given us, and we should enjoy all the great blessings He has given us here on earth. But above everything else, we should want to do things His way since He has given us life. Get a new attitude toward His commands and rules for life and love them and obey them, and they will give you a great life and relationship with God. God takes no pleasure in your choosing the wrong business/kingdom and the wrong boss—Satan or yourself.

— February 4

How I Can Do God's Will Today

_____

_____

_____

_____

_____

_____

_____

_____

_____

_____

_____

_____

_____

_____

_____

_____

_____

_____

_____

_____

_____

_____

_____

_____

_____

_____

_____

_____

_____

~ February 5

LEARN TO EXPECT TESTING

Be self-controlled and alert. Your enemy the devil prowls around like a roaring lion looking for someone to devour. Resist him, standing firm in the faith, because you know that your brothers throughout the world are undergoing the same kind of sufferings. And the God of all grace, who called you to his eternal glory in Christ, after you have suffered a little while, will himself restore you and make you strong, firm and steadfast.
— 1 Peter 5:8–10

Many times you feel like a failure, but if you will think with me, you will see that you are *not* a failure. Each day the evil forces want and tempt and lure you. They call your name in the morning, noon, and evening hours. In addition to that, God, Jesus, and all the heavenly beings are wooing you and courting you into God's presence with "happies" and jewels and rewards. *You are not a failure—rather, you are popular!* You have one dilemma—you must make a *choice.* However, if you just remember that God made you and Jesus saved you, you will see that you owe it all to God. Satan did not make you. Remind Satan that you are flattered, but you are going to give it all to God. When you are popular (your devotion is wanted), you must be self-controlled and alert!

~ February 6

HOW I CAN DO GOD'S WILL TODAY

— February 7

HIS NAME IS JEALOUS!

Do not worship any other god, for the LORD, whose name is Jealous, is a jealous God.

—Exodus 34:14

God Himself tells us that He is a jealous God, and yet we ignore this fact. But take a few minutes and really think about it. God is jealous of our hearts beating and racing in excitement for something that is on this earth, or in the heavens above, or in the waters below. Have you ever seen jealous husbands, wives, boyfriends, or girlfriends? They become dangerously jealous when they are afraid their loved ones have given their hearts away to others. Well, God displays this same emotion whenever you dream about getting alone with your extra food or other stronghold for a secret rendezvous. Anger and love are actually very near each other. My heart breaks for Him when I think about the many times He has gotten angry throughout the history of mankind when we have kissed something on this earth. We shouldn't think that He ignores what is happening. After all, we have learned from His own Word that He is a jealous God. His name is Jealous! Read about the idol of jealousy in Ezekiel 8–9.

HOW I CAN DO GOD'S WILL TODAY

February 1

LOVE GOD AND
ENJOY HIS FOOD

And God spoke all these words: "I am the LORD your God, who brought you out of Egypt, out of the land of slavery. You shall have no other gods before me."

—*Exodus* 20:1–3

Although God has put all foods on earth for us to enjoy, it is a very sad fact that too many Christians *love* the food and only *enjoy* God. Being overweight seems to have become accepted among some churchgoers. Many Bible studies and fellowship activities revolve around the food that is served. Again, God means for us to enjoy His wonderful variety of foods, but I'm here to tell you the truth: we must stop loving food and just enjoying God! Reverse this! *Love God,* and enjoy His food.

When we seek God first, a relationship is birthed, but God pulls back from the heart of the one who chooses other gods to adore. How could we have ever put God in second place? My friends, this cannot be. It is one thing to be caught red-handed one time with another lover—food—but many of us are repeatedly choosing to embrace it—sometimes secretly, other times in public. Many of us joke about it. We bring our secret loves into the only place in this world that is not supposed to have the world in it, the only place on earth where God asks for it to be just you and Him—your heart. Remember God's commandment to have no other gods before Him, and today start loving Him *first* and thankfully enjoying His many blessings on earth instead of loving food and only enjoying God.

—*February 10*

How I Can Do God's Will Today

_____
_____
_____
_____
_____
_____
_____
_____
_____
_____
_____
_____
_____
_____
_____
_____
_____
_____
_____
_____
_____
_____
_____
_____
_____
_____
_____
_____
_____

~ February 11

WHEN YOU TRULY LOVE, YOU WILL OBEY

Jesus replied, "If anyone loves me, he will obey my teaching. My Father will love him, and we will come to him and make our home with him. He who does not love me will not obey my teaching. These words you hear are not my own; they belong to the Father who sent me."

—John 14:23–24

"...the world must learn that I love the Father and that I do exactly what my Father has commanded me."

—John 14:31

If you love, love, love the Father and His precious Son, Jesus Christ, then you will not have any trouble obeying the Father today. It won't be work to obey; it will be a joy! After all, what boss could ever be more loving or more powerful or more all-knowing? Once you realize His love for you and recognize all the things He does for you each and every day, you will fall in love with Him. You will start seeing His words everywhere, and the invisible God will become more visible to you. But you must give your heart to Him in love first, and then the obedience to His commands will come naturally. What a barometer! If you rarely obey, you can be warned that you do not truly love God. Use this truth to be honest, repent, and then love, obey, and devote yourself to THE GOD of the universe. Through Jesus Christ, we have this awesome opportunity to turn toward God and show Him our love through our obedience.

— February 12

HOW I CAN DO GOD'S WILL TODAY

_____
_____
_____
_____
_____
_____
_____
_____
_____
_____
_____
_____
_____
_____
_____
_____
_____
_____
_____
_____
_____
_____
_____
_____
_____
_____
_____
_____
_____

—February 13

Exposing the
False God of Food

*Trust in the LORD and do good; dwell in the land and enjoy safe pasture.
Delight yourself in the LORD and he will give you the desires of your
heart.*

—Psalm 37:3–4

How can you leave food or other strongholds behind and dwell in the safe pasture of the Lord? Like the children of God who left Egypt, you need to know two things. First: Open your eyes to what a life-sucking leech the god of food is and what a life replenisher God is. Next: Take a crash course on how to fall in love with God.

First, let's expose this false god called food so that you can fall out of love with it. Just how good has excessive food been to you? Has bowing down to extra food helped your finances? No, it robs you as you spend more and more on food and diet plans. Has food clothed you? No, you probably find less and less to wear as you obey food more and more. Has it helped your self-esteem? No, the more that excessive food gathers on your hips and in other locations of the body, the more your self-esteem drops. Does it help your relationships? No, it often puts a wedge between you and your family or spouse. Does it help your looks? No, in fact, being overweight distorts the looks that God gave you. So you see, the god of food turns out to be a false, parasitic leech that robs you of time, passion, money, devotion, peace, and self-esteem. It is a false master that leaves you with increasing troubles, guilt, emotional deprivation, and physical ailments. It cannot give back to you or return your love.

Realize what a loving, generous, powerful, and attractive God our Lord is. He can provide anything and everything for you. He can lift your self-esteem, fix your finances, and strengthen your relationships. He is the one true God, and following only Him will give you real peace and contentment as you finally realize the desires of your heart.

~ February 14

HOW I CAN DO GOD'S WILL TODAY

~ February 15

ACTIONS AND FAITH
WORK TOGETHER

What good is it, my brothers, if a man claims to have faith but has no deeds? Can such faith save him? . . . You foolish man, do you want evidence that faith without deeds is useless? Was not our ancestor Abraham considered righteous for what he did when he offered his son Isaac on the altar? You see that his faith and his actions were working together, and his faith was made complete by what he did. And the scripture was fulfilled that says, "Abraham believed God, and it was credited to him as righteousness," and he was called God's friend. You see that a person is justified by what he does and not by faith alone.

—James 2:14, 20–24

What good is it if a man claims to have faith but has no deeds or actions to back it up? Can such a faith *save* him? Well, the answer is no. Abraham was willing to—and almost did—kill his only son for God. He did not question the Boss's decision to kill a child—and not just any child—his dearest child from old age. Abraham didn't talk back; he didn't try to talk God out of it; he didn't trump the decision and explain later. No, he was presented with the ultimate test, and *he obeyed*. Why? Because he feared, loved, trusted, and entrusted himself to the Great CEO of the world. This is the faith that saves. God will test your heart and analyze your actions, for "you see that a person is justified by what he *does* and not by faith alone."

— February 16

How I Can Do God's Will Today

— February 17

TREASURE HIS WORDS

I have treasured the words of his mouth more than my daily bread.

—Job 23:12b

Your statutes are wonderful; therefore I obey them. The unfolding of your words gives light; it gives understanding to the simple. I open my mouth and pant, longing for your commands. Turn to me and have mercy on me, as you always do to those who love your name. Direct my footsteps according to your word; let no sin rule over me. Redeem me from the oppression of men, that I may obey your precepts. Make your face shine upon your servant and teach me your decrees. Streams of tears flow from my eyes, for your law is not obeyed.

—Psalm 119:129–136

I share Job's feelings in the verse from the book bearing his name because I treasure the words of God's mouth more than my daily bread. I do not have a one-way relationship with the Father. I have a two-way conversation, even though I do not hear a voice audibly. I stay in the Word to hear His voice, and I have several identical Bibles that I like to use. The only time I panic is when I think I have left my Bible at home after setting out on a trip. God's guidance is everything to me, and I want to know what He thinks. He keeps my foot from stumbling, He gives me wisdom for which direction to turn, and He protects me from the enemy. I have to have His Word, and I love His laws because they are always right! Do you have a question about a principle? The answer is in God's Word.

~ February 18

How I Can Do God's Will Today

— February 11

For Yours Is the Kingdom

"'Our Father in heaven, hallowed be your name, your kingdom come, your will be done on earth as it is in heaven. Give us today our daily bread. Forgive us our debts, as we also have forgiven our debtors. And lead us not into temptation, but deliver us from the evil one.'"

—Matthew 6:9b–13

Jesus taught us how to pray, and I believe His heart was saying the following:

Dear Heavenly Father:

Hallowed be Your name. (Hallowed and awesome and incredible and most deserving be Your name; You are a Genius beyond genius.)

Your kingdom come. (We pray that Your ideas, Your truths, Your government, Your justice, and Your ways to live replace this worldly way of life because Your kingdom is perfect.)

Give us today our daily bread. (Give us this day the portion we need.)

Lead us not into temptation. (May we not be tempted today. After all, this is not our kingdom—it is Yours.)

But deliver us from the evil one. (Deliver us from Satan, who is constantly misrepresenting You and falsely accusing You. We know that You are perfect in all Your leadership.)

For Yours is the kingdom, the power, and the glory forever. (After all, You are it. You are everything. You are all-powerful. You are who we worship, admire, and adore.)

Amen.

~ February 20

HOW I CAN DO GOD'S WILL TODAY

— February 21

THE CREATED
VERSUS THE CREATOR

*They exchanged the truth of God for a lie, and worshiped and served
created things rather than the Creator—who is forever praised. Amen.*
                                                    —Romans 1:25

We human beings have a tendency to worship the *created* and
not the *Creator*. We worship things because of the temporary
pleasures they give us, but we ignore the One who made us capable
of feeling that pleasure. We are so quick to fall in love with an object
because of its beauty or its capability, but we fail to recognize that the
Father created that beauty and that capability even before the object
was formed.

God is jealous of our attention to and adoration of the things that
He has made. How can we get so confused that we forget that God
made everything on this earth? He made our senses (smell, sight,
hearing, touch, taste) so that we would experience and celebrate His
genius, and He gave us these things on earth to enjoy. Let's stop
being confused and start showing God our full, undivided appreciation instead of ignoring Him in favor of His creations. He deserves
so much more than what He asks for. How humble of Him to
demand so little, and yet we do not bother to give Him what little
He asks for. Please read the rest of Romans 1 to consider the plight
of those who choose such an unappreciative attitude.

~ February 22

HOW I CAN DO GOD'S WILL TODAY

~ February 23

A SUPERIOR INVITATION

What then? Shall we sin because we are not under law but under grace? By no means! Don't you know that when you offer yourselves to someone to obey him as slaves, you are slaves to the one whom you obey— whether you are slaves to sin, which leads to death, or to obedience, which leads to righteousness? But thanks be to God that, though you used to be slaves to sin, you wholeheartedly obeyed the form of teaching to which you were entrusted. You have been set free from sin and have become slaves to righteousness.

—Romans 6:15–18

We should not abuse grace, and we should not embarrass God in front of all the celestial world by running after other lovers on this earth. We have the opportunity, given through God's grace and mercy alone, to accept a covenant offered by God that is similar to a marriage proposal. He has made the offer and the provisions through Jesus Christ to cross the tracks, since we live on the wrong side of the tracks. Through Jesus Christ, we can approach the throne, and we have the opportunity to be employees of the most powerful CEO in the universe. What you do to chase down the best mate . . . what you do to get the best job—open your eyes: you've been offered both! No longer run after other things—run after God. That's how to accept grace and no longer continue in sin. It's that simple! Accept His kind proposal. Put your hands to the plow and do *not* look back. Paul was saying that you are a slave to either sin or obedience, and you used to be a slave to sin but now you are a slave to doing right or righteousness. Read Psalm 119 and listen to how the psalmist *loved* to fully obey God. I continue to grow happier and happier as I follow the same path.

— February 24

HOW I CAN DO GOD'S WILL TODAY

— February 25

A Sign of His Goodness

Turn to me and have mercy on me; grant your strength to your servant and save the son of your maidservant. Give me a sign of your goodness, that my enemies may see it and be put to shame, for you, O LORD, have helped me and comforted me.

—Psalm 86:16–17

It is okay to call out to God and ask Him to show you that He is there for you. There are times when we all need this reassurance. It is also okay to call upon Him for your needs. After all, He wants you to see His glorious works for you so that you will experience the direct relationship between your request and His answer. This will help you develop pure trust that He can and will take care of you. Ask for a sign of His goodness today, and be prepared to be awed!

Physical reassurance builds our faith. I have never found God to get upset when we ask for evidence of His love; however, scriptures indicate that God does not like unbelievers to *keep* asking for signs to prove His existence (Matthew 16:1–4). How annoying that must be to God! We see the stars, His handiwork, His sunsets that have a different color scheme daily, and we witness the birth of new life. Yet some *still* demand a miraculous sign to prove the existence of God. Please! God is tired of showing off in such fantastic ways and hearing people continue to demand a sign to prove His existence. But for the person pursuing a loving relationship with God, He provides whatever it takes to make His beloved secure in His presence. Asking for reassurance from God is not testing God—it is *seeking* God. That is His command for us.

~ February 26

How I Can Do God's Will Today

_____
_____
_____
_____
_____
_____
_____
_____
_____
_____
_____
_____
_____
_____
_____
_____
_____
_____
_____
_____
_____
_____
_____
_____
_____
_____
_____
_____
_____

~ February 27

STEP OUT IN FAITH

He led you through the vast and dreadful desert, that thirsty and water-
less land, with its venomous snakes and scorpions.

—*Deuteronomy* 8:15a

The desert is described in the Bible as "vast and dreadful, thirsty
and waterless, with snakes and scorpions." As you entered this
place and things started to get tough, you may have been tempted to
return to Egypt and the slavery of dieting. In the beginning, you
learned that your *mind* was focused on food more than you knew.
Then, you found out that your *heart* was given to food, too. How do
I know? Because in my years of counseling, I've learned that everyone has felt the tug-of-war—the major battles going on for the heart.
If you had just been missing information, one week in Weigh Down*
would have done it. But you never realized that making a choice to
turn to God was going to be hard to do. My advice—step out in faith,
as you would on a blind date. God will be better than a binge, but
you have to go out and taste and see that He is good. And to do that,
you have to leave some food behind and step into the desert. I trust
God. The desert is so much better than the world!

— February 28

DESERT JOURNEY

HOW I CAN DO GOD'S WILL TODAY

March 7

OBEY THE LORD'S ORDER

Whenever the cloud lifted from above the Tent, the Israelites set out; wherever the cloud settled, the Israelites encamped. At the LORD's command the Israelites set out, and at his command they encamped. As long as the cloud stayed over the tabernacle, they remained in camp. When the cloud remained over the tabernacle a long time, the Israelites obeyed the LORD's order and did not set out. Sometimes the cloud was over the tabernacle only a few days; at the LORD's command they would encamp, and then at his command they would set out. Sometimes the cloud stayed only from evening till morning, and when it lifted in the morning, they set out. Whether by day or by night, whenever the cloud lifted, they set out. Whether the cloud stayed over the tabernacle for two days or a month or a year, the Israelites would remain in camp and not set out; but when it lifted, they would set out. At the LORD's command they encamped, and at the LORD's command they set out. They obeyed the LORD's order, in accordance with his command through Moses.

—Numbers 9:17–23

After the parting of the Red Sea, the children of God followed a cloud by day and a fire by night. No matter whether the cloud stayed two days, a month, or a year, the Israelites would remain in camp. But when the cloud lifted, they would set out again. Think about this if you start feeling sorry that you have to look to God to know when you are hungry and when you are full. The Israelites had to look up *all day* and *all night*. Even in the middle of the night, they had to pack the tents, put out the fires, gather children and animals, and take off. Sometimes, just after they had unpacked their belongings, set up the tent, and had a good pot of manna boiling, God lifted the cloud, and they had to pack everything up and take off again. We should stop complaining about the red light and green light of hunger. All *you* will have to pack up is a carryout of food! Remember, we are blessed to have the breath of life at all! We owe our God our entire attention. The amounts of food He gives are *generous!*

—March 2

HOW I CAN DO GOD'S WILL TODAY

March 3

GOD HEARS OUR CRIES

Then they cried out to the LORD in their trouble, and he delivered them from their distress.

—Psalm 107:6

If you read the Psalms in full, you will see that most of the psalmist's cries were for God to punish the mocking people who made fun of him because his ways were blameless (Psalm 119:1–3). The sinner taunts those who obey God's decrees. God promised to dig pitfalls for the wicked. But when you are starting this Exodus, you will learn to cry out to God.

At one time, God's children were free men in a foreign land. But once God saw they had become slaves and were forced to make bricks for Egypt, He heard their cries, and He fought a mighty battle for the deliverance of the Israelites. God is now fighting for the deliverance of your heart so that you will no longer experience an attraction to things on this earth. He can deliver your heart from the distress of any addiction because His attraction is much stronger than the earth's attraction. You start your Exodus by crying out to God to rescue you and keep your eyes focused on Him, and then you will experience His mighty deliverance. Read the Psalms.

March 4

HOW I CAN DO GOD'S WILL TODAY

_____

_____

_____

_____

_____

_____

_____

_____

_____

_____

_____

_____

_____

_____

_____

_____

_____

_____

_____

_____

_____

_____

_____

_____

_____

_____

_____

_____

_____

_____

March 5

GOD SPEAKS TENDERLY TO US

"Therefore I am now going to allure her; I will lead her into the desert and speak tenderly to her. There I will give her back her vineyards, and will make the Valley of Achor [trouble] a door of hope. There she will sing as in the days of her youth, as in the day she came up out of Egypt. In that day," declares the LORD, *"you will call me 'my husband'; you will no longer call me 'my master.' I will remove the names of the Baals from her lips; no longer will their names be invoked."*

—Hosea 2:14–17

When you turn back to God and away from food, God will reward you. He will turn your past troubles (Valley of Achor) into a door of hope and happiness. You see, God is a genius of behavior modification. He knows that as humans, we would rather do the things that will bring us happiness, and what better happiness and peace than that offered by the Creator of the universe? Our loving Father loves to reward us when we choose to spend time adoring and worshiping Him instead of mere earthly things. God wants to allure us, to lead us, and to speak tenderly to us. What earthly idol can compare to that? When you fall in love with God, you will no longer call for or call upon your stronghold. In that way, God removes the names of your idols from your lips. We must think very hard about our hearts if we ignore such an opportunity.

March 6

HOW I CAN DO GOD'S WILL TODAY

March 7

YOU ARE NOT A GOD

This is what the Sovereign LORD says: "In the pride of your heart you say, 'I am a god; I sit on the throne of a god in the heart of the seas.' But you are a man and not a god, though you think you are as wise as a god."

—*Ezekiel 28:2b*

Face it. If something is going wrong, you have become your own boss again. The Bible tells us that if we remain connected to God, everything we need will be given to us. If things are going wrong, let this be a sign to you to reexamine your relationship with the Father. Don't you *want* to let Him guide you today? Either you do or you don't. If you *do*, you will find happiness. After all, God knows the past, present, and future, and He loves you and wants the best for you. Who better to give you advice? When you step down and let God be God, you will have such peace, and you will be amazed at the gifts He gives His submissive children. It is so fun! But if you *don't*, if you think you are wiser than God and can decide for Him how much and when to eat, who and when to lust sexually for, or how much money you will have, then you are *arrogant*. Think hard and remember who made you and who has given you everything! *Humility* will be the result, and God esteems and takes care of the humble!

March 8

HOW I CAN DO GOD'S WILL TODAY

March 1

AN EVEN GREATER ENEMY THAN PHARAOH

For the LORD brought you out of Egypt with his mighty hand.
—*Exodus 13:9b*

God rescued the Israelites from the slavery of this earth, and what a battle it was! He took them into the desert so He could win the heart of man with no earthly competition. However, He found that the desert brought forth a more ominous competition—the god of self. The Israelites kept crying out, "Why have You brought us up out of Egypt to die in the desert? Why have You brought us up out of Egypt to die in the desert?" That is the point exactly: God brought them out to die ... *to die to their wills.* But the desert seemed to revive the will of man, making it stronger than it was while under the burden of slavery to the earth!

The will of man was thriving, not dying as planned. Suffering in the desert was not killing the craving of man. You may have found a greater battle going on in the desert than you have ever felt before. The will of man seems to have an independent heartbeat of its own, and it has no intention of learning trust in the one true Lord as long as this little god's heart is beating. What foolish pride we have! But the cloud of God stayed over the rebellious hearts of the Israelites, patiently watching to see if anyone would consider joining the kingdom of which He is the Boss.

March 10

How I Can Do God's Will Today

March 11

FOOD IS NOT YOUR BOSS

But now that you have been set free from sin and have become slaves to God, the benefit you reap leads to holiness, and the result is eternal life.
—Romans 6:22

Romans 6:16 tells us that we are slaves to the one whom we obey. Up until now, you have been a slave to food, or money, or sexual lust, or sports, or television. But what a wonderful opportunity you now have! You have been set free. You are no longer a slave to any of these worldly things. When food or anything of the world calls your name today, you can say, "No! *You* are not my boss!" What a great freedom to have only one Master, our awesome God Almighty! The result is life—so get a life!

March 12

How I Can Do God's Will Today

March 13

GUARD YOUR SOUL

In the paths of the wicked lie thorns and snares, but he who guards his soul stays far from them.

—Proverbs 22:5

Rejoice in the Lord always. I will say it again: Rejoice! Let your gentleness be evident to all. The Lord is near. Do not be anxious about anything, but in everything, by prayer and petition, with thanksgiving, present your requests to God. And the peace of God, which transcends all understanding, will guard your hearts and your minds in Christ Jesus.

—Philippians 4:4–7

Guard your heart from evil thoughts. Make sure your heart and mind do not linger on the thoughts that will lead you astray. Sin can take root in our hearts and grow strong if we are not careful. In Mark 7:20–23, Jesus said: "What comes out of a man is what makes him 'unclean.' For from within, out of men's hearts, come evil thoughts, sexual immorality, theft, murder, adultery, greed, malice, deceit, lewdness, envy, slander, arrogance and folly. All these evils come from inside and make a man 'unclean.'" We should always be careful to protect ourselves within. Set your mind on things above. Keep your heart busy by focusing on God's business and what He is doing, and you will reap great reward. Be careful, eyes, what you see, and be careful, ears, what you hear; God's will and Word will guard your soul!

March 14

HOW I CAN DO GOD'S WILL TODAY

March 15

THE LORD WILL FIGHT FOR YOU

As Pharaoh approached, the Israelites looked up, and there were the
Egyptians, marching after them. They were terrified and cried out to the
LORD . . . Moses answered the people, "Do not be afraid. Stand firm
and you will see the deliverance the LORD will bring you today. The
Egyptians you see today you will never see again. The LORD will fight
for you; you need only to be still." Then the LORD said to Moses, "Why
are you crying out to me? Tell the Israelites to move on. Raise your staff
and stretch out your hand over the sea to divide the water so that the
Israelites can go through the sea on dry ground."

—Exodus 14:10, 13–16

When Satan comes with his temptations and personal attacks,
trying to lure you back to Egypt or get you discouraged with
choosing the best Boss and kingdom, please stand firm and call out
to God. Do not plan to defend yourself. Just run to God, and watch
Him defeat the enemy. He will defend you. Quit worrying about
Egypt and the Egyptians and Satan, for you'll never see them again if
you allow God to defend you. If you are spending your energy living
in fear of the attacks of Satan, then you are not focused on God. You
can't be in both camps. Now, if you want to stand firm in the desert,
what do you need to do? You need to move on! Get going! Pursue
God with all your might, and He will lead you safely. All of the
people of God—those who were humble before Him and afraid not
to pursue a "blameless" life (Psalm 119:1–3)—were taunted and
mocked by the religious who did not want to submit totally to God
(Psalm 119:42). Read Psalm 119 in full and underline the word *arro-*
gant or *wicked*, and notice that with each attack, the psalmist
answered, "But I do not turn from your law [Word]" or "But I obey
your law." The answer to attacks is to stay focused on God, stay in
the Word and obey it, and the Lord will put your enemies down.

—March 16

HOW I CAN DO GOD'S WILL TODAY

March 17

"Esau I Hated"

Just as it is written: "Jacob I loved, but Esau I hated."
—Romans 9:13

See that no one . . . is godless like Esau, who for a single meal sold his inheritance rights as the oldest son.
—Hebrews 12:16

When I was a young girl, I wondered what it meant when God said, "Jacob I loved, but Esau I hated." Did Jacob not lie and cheat to get his brother's birthright? Is that okay with God? As I got older, I understood this better. Now I understand that Jacob was crazy about God, and he would do anything to obtain the birthright because this inheritance would make him even closer to God. Esau, on the other hand, was willing to sell his priceless birthright for a bowl of stew! Think about it: Esau traded being close to God for food! Does this sound familiar to you? Esau is called "godless" in the book of Hebrews, where we are cautioned not to be like him.

God loves the child who wants to get closer to Him or get in good with Him, and He will reward your efforts. I do not get mad at my dogs, Chaucer and Virginia, for fighting over getting close to me. God loved Jacob for doing everything he could to get close to God's heart. To most people, Esau looked sinless, and Jacob looked like a sinner. But think again. Sin is not loving God fully and wholeheartedly, and it can be manifested in many ways—just as seeking the Father can be.

March 18

How I Can Do God's Will Today

March 11

LOVE GOD FIRST,
THEN EVERYONE ELSE

This is the message you heard from the beginning: We should love one another. Do not be like Cain, who belonged to the evil one and murdered his brother. And why did he murder him? Because his own actions were evil and his brother's were righteous. Do not be surprised, my brothers, if the world hates you. We know that we have passed from death to life, because we love our brothers. Anyone who does not love remains in death. Anyone who hates his brother is a murderer, and you know that no murderer has eternal life in him. This is how we know what love is: Jesus Christ laid down his life for us. And we ought to lay down our lives for our brothers.

— 1 John 3:11–16

God has shown us clearly through the Ten Commandments that He wants us to love and honor Him above all else. Jesus stated that we should love God and then love our fellowman as ourselves— in that order. You see, when you have the relationship in which God is your heart's foremost desire, then, and only then, can you love and honor mankind the way you should. After all, if you love God and believe that He created and cares for everyone on the earth, how could you hurt one of the children that He loves? That would be unnatural! Notice the real reason that anyone would hate anyone on this earth—because the actions of the others are righteous and their own actions are evil (or rebellious to God). Do you despise people in Weigh Down*t* who are being obedient to God? Do you feel hated by the world? Both questions reveal your heart's position. Think about it.

March 20

How I Can Do God's Will Today

March 21

THE GREATEST DEFENDER

The LORD says to my Lord: "Sit at my right hand until I make your enemies a footstool for your feet."

—*Psalm 110:1*

Do not take revenge, my friends, but leave room for God's wrath, for it is written: "It is mine to avenge; I will repay," says the Lord.

—*Romans 12:19*

Instead of trying to defend yourself, let God defend you. I have witnessed God setting my enemies down again and again. I define an enemy as one who attacks me as I try to serve the Lord and follow His will. If the enemy can make you look bad or falsely accuse you in front of others, then the attack can potentially stop God's sheep from seeing the truth about how easy it is to come to the Father. God certainly does not want this to happen.

I have seen God fight. He is a brilliant strategist and the best of the best generals in war. Enemies of those who truly love God should watch out, for it is God's to avenge, and He will repay! Keep your battle armor on, but let God do the avenging.

March 22

HOW I CAN DO GOD'S WILL TODAY

March 23

THE STOMACH GOD

Join with others in following my example, brothers, and take note of those who live according to the pattern we gave you. For, as I have often told you before and now say again even with tears, many live as enemies of the cross of Christ. Their destiny is destruction, their god is their stomach, and their glory is in their shame. Their mind is on earthly things. But our citizenship is in heaven. And we eagerly await a Savior from there, the Lord Jesus Christ, who, by the power that enables him to bring everything under his control, will transform our lowly bodies so that they will be like his glorious body.

—Philippians 3:17–21

An enemy of the cross of Christ has his stomach as his god. Does this hit home? Don't let your stomach be your god. You will only get larger and larger with this type of worship. And as you grow larger, so will your desire; it will never be satisfied. And think about it: your *stomach*—what a stupid god to bow down to! People who do this run over others as they lust and live for the "feedings" every day. Get your focus off your stomach, and let it do the job God meant for it to do. Instead, focus on the wonderful spiritual food that God provides—the satisfying nutrition of an interactive, totally submissive relationship with Him! Take hold of your citizenship in heaven, and mold your heart to be more like the heart of our heavenly Father.

March 24

HOW I CAN DO GOD'S WILL TODAY

March 25

WHAT DO YOU WORRY ABOUT?

"Who of you by worrying can add a single hour to his life? And why do you worry about clothes? See how the lilies of the field grow. They do not labor or spin. Yet I tell you that not even Solomon in all his splendor was dressed like one of these. If that is how God clothes the grass of the field, which is here today and tomorrow is thrown into the fire, will he not much more clothe you, O you of little faith? So do not worry, saying, 'What shall we eat?' or 'What shall we drink?' or 'What shall we wear?' For the pagans run after all these things, and your heavenly Father knows that you need them. But seek first his kingdom and his righteousness, and all these things will be given to you as well. Therefore do not worry about tomorrow, for tomorrow will worry about itself. Each day has enough trouble of its own."

—Matthew 6:27–34

What you worry about is your idol. Do you worry about your children, or your spouse, or your health? These are common idols. Shift your worry and concern and energy into worrying about God's children more than your own children. Too many of God's children are lost and underfed or emaciated spiritually. Their spiritual health is the worst. They are dying of spiritual cancers, and they have spiritually clogged arteries. Make *this* your worry and God will be sure to please you beyond what you could think or imagine or dream. Worry more about His business than your own business. Really mean it when you say "*Your* kingdom come." In other words, you really mean "Your business take over and rule all other businesses, nations, governments, and kingdoms." Pray that God takes over what is rightfully His—starting with your heart. Worry about that and everything else will come to you!

March 26

How I Can Do God's Will Today

March 27

KEEPING GOD NEAR

Righteous are you, O LORD, and your laws are right. The statutes you have laid down are righteous; they are fully trustworthy. My zeal wears me out, for my enemies ignore your words. Your promises have been thoroughly tested, and your servant loves them. Though I am lowly and despised, I do not forget your precepts. Your righteousness is everlasting and your law is true. Trouble and distress have come upon me, but your commands are my delight. Your statutes are forever right; give me understanding that I may live.

—Psalm 119:137–144

The psalmist was always thinking about God, whether he was praying to Him or singing songs of appreciation, joy, or sorrow to Him. We, too, should meditate on God's law all day long. One way to do this is to keep God's Word by you at all times. I keep a copy of the Bible with me everywhere I go, and my heart quickens when I think I can get some time alone with God. I talk to Him all the time, not just in formal prayers. No matter who I am with or where I am, I know that God would come if I needed Him, and I know that He keeps angels nearby. Trust in God's superior knowledge and love, and have faith that His guidance will make you wiser, happier, and more fulfilled. Ignore the words and call of food and its labels. It will only prove to be a trap that will grab you and never let you go.

March 28

How I Can Do God's Will Today

_____

_____

_____

_____

_____

_____

_____

_____

_____

_____

_____

_____

_____

_____

_____

_____

_____

_____

_____

_____

_____

_____

_____

_____

_____

_____

_____

_____

_____

_____

_____

_____

_____

_____

_____

_____

_____

March 21

JOHN THE BAPTIST
PREPARES THE WAY

In those days John the Baptist came, preaching in the Desert of Judea and saying, "Repent, for the kingdom of heaven is near." This is he who was spoken of through the prophet Isaiah: "A voice of one calling in the desert, 'Prepare the way for the Lord, make straight paths for him.'"

—*Matthew 3:1–3*

When John the Baptist told people how to prepare for heaven, he told them to *repent*. John was preparing the way for the Lord by telling people to repent. Why is repentance so important? Well, repentance is not only the key to unlocking the heart of *man*, but it is also the key to unlocking *God's* heartstrings. True repentance unlocks the heart of man by cleaning out the heart of its impurities, making it humble and open to God's commands in recognition of the Lord's sovereignty. True repentance unlocks God's heartstrings by showing God that you are ready to accept His will and His decisions and His commands. It says to God, "I know that You are the best for me, and I want to throw away my impurities and serve You in obedience." Your heart cannot house your old goals *and* your new goals. Repent, and have one sweet goal: following Jesus Christ all the way to the heart of the Father!

March 30

HOW I CAN DO GOD'S WILL TODAY

March 31

GOD IS YOUR EVERYTHING

He said to me: "It is done. I am the Alpha and the Omega, the Beginning and the End. To him who is thirsty I will give to drink without cost from the spring of the water of life. He who overcomes will inherit all this, and I will be his God and he will be my son."

—Revelation 21:6–7

And my God will meet all your needs according to his glorious riches in Christ Jesus.

—Philippians 4:19

Our days are busy. We work; we raise a family; we have too many things to do each day. We spend a lot of time worrying about all the things we need to do, but we really shouldn't worry. When you are focused on God and looking to Him to help you do your job, help you raise the children, and help you with your marriage, you will experience how He takes care of everything you have been worried about. If you give everything to God, including every daily activity and worry, He will provide for you in large ways and small ways. You will find that suddenly it seems that you are able to achieve so much more than you thought you could. If you stay focused on God, His kingdom (or His business), and His desires, then you will find that He is your *Alpha* and *Omega*. He is the Beginning and the End. He is everything and provides everything!

—April 7

How I Can Do God's Will Today

April R

"EACH ONE IS TO GATHER AS MUCH AS HE NEEDS"

"This is what the LORD has commanded: 'Each one is to gather as much as he needs'"... Then Moses said to them, "No one is to keep any of it until morning." However, some of them paid no attention to Moses; they kept part of it until morning, but it was full of maggots and began to smell. So Moses was angry with them.

—*Exodus 16:16a, 19–20*

Food was made to be a tool to serve mankind, not man to be the slave of food! It is not wrong to leave food behind on your plate. If it rots or is wasted, so what! God has more for you. When God sent manna to the Israelites in the desert, He sent them more than they needed to be satisfied. But He told them not to be greedy and not to gather more than they needed for that day. Notice that the Lord commanded each to gather as much as he *needs*, not as much as his head wants or as much as his neighbor gathers. We need to trust God to provide our daily bread, which He will supply each and every day. Do not show a lack of faith in His completely competent care by being greedy or by getting yourself extra food as if there will be no food for tomorrow. Do not let yourself or your children be slaves to leftovers. Let's learn from the Israelites' example—have faith that God will give you what you need.

Also remember that the amount *needed* is generous! Stop crying about eating only three times per day. God could have set it up so that we got to eat only once every *five days*. God is very generous. Please praise Him every day.

April 3

HOW I CAN DO GOD'S WILL TODAY

April 4

CLOUD BY DAY, FIRE BY NIGHT

*By day the LORD went ahead of them in a pillar of cloud to guide them
on their way and by night in a pillar of fire to give them light, so that they
could travel by day or night. Neither the pillar of cloud by day nor the
pillar of fire by night left its place in front of the people.*

—Exodus 13:21–22

*"But when he, the Spirit of truth, comes, he will guide you into all truth.
He will not speak on his own; he will speak only what he hears, and he
will tell you what is yet to come."*

—John 16:13

After God parted the Red Sea and delivered the Israelites from
the slavery of Egypt, scripture tells us that He went ahead of
them in the form of a cloud by day and a fire by night. The cloud
never left their sides the entire forty years in the desert, no matter
what they did to God—and they did some pretty wicked things. God
is still with us today—actually closer than the cloud, since He has
sent the Holy Spirit to us to guide us into all truths. How attentive
can you get? No other being has been so kind, and because of His personal care, I love Him! Open up all of your senses to learn His leading. Please never take it for granted that you have the opportunity to
choose to be under His guidance or Satan's. Please choose humbly
and wisely—choose God. Oh, what grace that allows us this opportunity!

—April 5

How I Can Do God's Will Today

April 6

FEEDING HIS LAMBS

When they had finished eating, Jesus said to Simon Peter, "Simon son of John, do you truly love me more than these?" "Yes, Lord," he said, "you know that I love you." Jesus said, "Feed my lambs." Again Jesus said, "Simon son of John, do you truly love me?" He answered, "Yes, Lord, you know that I love you." Jesus said, "Take care of my sheep." The third time he said to him, "Simon son of John, do you love me?" Peter was hurt because Jesus asked him the third time, "Do you love me?" He said, "Lord, you know all things; you know that I love you." Jesus said, "Feed my sheep."

—John 21:15–17

What is the key to showing our love for the Father? The answer is here: focus on God and His sheep. Jesus wants His lambs—His followers, those who are seeking to know more about Him—to be fed and not to go hungry for the knowledge of Him or for His love and His will. Jesus wants us who love and care for Him to love and care for others in the world, for *all* are His lambs. In fact, we should be more concerned about feeding His sheep than feeding ourselves, for we know that God will take care of us! To feed followers of Christ would be to feed them truth that helps them turn from wrong paths and turn toward the true path of facing the cross daily and denying themselves daily. You will be persecuted if you are helping to gain more territory for God's rule by helping others get their will out of the way. But *blessed* are they who are persecuted for Christ's sake. We have already learned from Jesus that if we love God, we will obey His commands. Obey the command Jesus gave to Simon, and then write to me (the address can be found in the back of this book) and let me know of the secret heartfelt joy this focus brings to you today!

—April 7

HOW I CAN DO GOD'S WILL TODAY

April 8

ARE YOU BACKSTROKING THE RED SEA?

Therefore, prepare your minds for action; be self-controlled; set your hope fully on the grace to be given you when Jesus Christ is revealed. As obedient children, do not conform to the evil desires you had when you lived in ignorance. But just as he who called you is holy, so be holy in all you do; for it is written: "Be holy, because I am holy."

— 1 Peter 1:13–16

If we find ourselves in the pantry and refrigerator night after night, we are still in the arms of Egypt. But I'm afraid the deceiver has told us that we have made God our choice and that we have left our slavery. Even after the mighty Exodus, many of us have slowly done the backstroke across the Red Sea and wound up back on the shoreline of Egypt. We are actually back in Egypt, but this time, it has been redecorated so that we will not recognize it. Where once there were pyramids, there are now church pews and stained glass windows. We have brought the world into the church, the one place where only we and God should be. Listen to what Peter wrote: "As obedient children, do not conform to the evil desires you had when you lived in ignorance." Do not backstroke across the Red Sea to Egypt's shore. We need to start now to help clean up the church (and our hearts) for God! God warned us through His preacher-prophet Isaiah, "'Woe to the obstinate children,' declares the LORD, 'to those who carry out plans that are not mine ... heaping sin upon sin; who go down to Egypt ... who look for help to Pharaoh's protection, to Egypt's shade for refuge ... This sin will become for you like a high wall, cracked and bulging, that collapses suddenly, in an instant'" (Isaiah 30:1–2, 13).

—April 9

HOW I CAN DO GOD'S WILL TODAY

April 10

WELCOMING THE FATHER

An argument started among the disciples as to which of them would be the greatest. Jesus, knowing their thoughts, took a little child and had him stand beside him. Then he said to them, "Whoever welcomes this little child in my name welcomes me; and whoever welcomes me welcomes the one who sent me. For he who is least among you all—he is the greatest."

—Luke 9:46–48

This passage means that the less you think you have and the more you rely on God, the more you will get. The one who is least usually has no problem with trying to be a god and has no problem with pride. These are the conditions that will leave room for the holy and separate Spirit of God to come in and not have to mix with your own will. So if we welcome the little ones into the kingdom, then we are welcoming the Father in!

In Luke 10:21b, Jesus became full of joy through the Holy Spirit, and He proclaimed, "I praise you, Father, Lord of heaven and earth, because you have hidden these things from the wise and learned, and revealed them to little children. Yes, Father, for this was your good pleasure." I just love this passage because it shows the love of God for the priceless heart. People who have no need for God cannot please God. Those of us who know that we need Him every hour of every day are like little children. This humble childlike heart is the heart that fits right in with the perfectly powerful but humble kingdom of God.

—April 11

How I Can Do God's Will Today

April 12

SINKING AND SAVING

But when he saw the wind, he was afraid and, beginning to sink, cried out, "Lord, save me!" Immediately Jesus reached out his hand and caught him. "You of little faith," he said, "why did you doubt?"

—Matthew 14:30–31

If you trust God to feed you, you naturally will not focus on the food at all. A person could *believe* that God will provide, but to *trust* Him fully means that you are happy with the amount of food He gives you. In fact, you cannot get over the fact that He lets you eat sweet and salty foods every day. He could have made everything tasteless! You trust that this amount of food is the best for your heart, soul, and body, even if the amount is a lot smaller than you would have chosen for yourself. The person who does *not* fully trust God to provide, however, will feel obligated to focus on food all throughout the day. The next thing you know, he is unsure about weight loss and is back on the scales; he grows uneasy about eating regular foods, and he is back to counting fat grams and calories. This lack of trust in God's total reign could send you back down a path of slavery of self-employment or being your own god. Yuck! If that happens, you will find that you have totally lost your focus, and like Peter, you are sinking in the water. Follow Peter's example—call out to Jesus to save you. Your sinking and His saving are part of the process that Jesus will allow as He trains you in obedience.

April 13

How I Can Do God's Will Today

April 94

"Arrogant, Overfed and Unconcerned"

"'Now this was the sin of your sister Sodom: She and her daughters were arrogant, overfed and unconcerned; they did not help the poor and needy. They were haughty and did detestable things before me. Therefore I did away with them as you have seen.'"

—Ezekiel 16:49–50

I believe there are many obstacles to overcome when you turn your whole heart purely to the Father. But nothing worries me more than the attitude of *unconcern*. People who don't know the truth don't have the opportunity to surface an unconcerned attitude. But after you have been told the truth about your heart wandering to food, then you should feel saddened and guilty, much like the thief on the cross who said, "We deserve what we are getting." The book of Ezekiel marries the word *unconcerned* with *overfed*. Something tells me if we would not overeat, then we would develop more and more concern about our relationship with the Father. When we release our hearts from being enslaved to an idol, we can give our hearts to whom they belong: to God. The last associated word is *arrogant*. You probably do not consider yourself arrogant, but if you have remained overweight for a while, you *do* have all of these qualities because you think you don't need to obey God as other people do. You consider yourself special. But believe me—you don't want to be arrogant, overfed, and unconcerned. Join me and many others and change your heart today into a fearfully concerned attitude that does not feel as if it deserves to eat—much less more than what the God of the universe has allotted.

~April 15

How I Can Do God's Will Today

April 16

TRY HIM AND SEE

"Test me in this," says the LORD *Almighty, "and see if I will not throw open the floodgates of heaven and pour out so much blessing that you will not have room enough for it."*

—Malachi 3:10b

We cannot run to false gods to get us out of our pain, and we cannot save ourselves by building golden calves in the form of diet pills, liposuction, diet programs, hospital liquid diets, and fat farms. Let's get serious by giving our hearts, our souls, our minds, and our strength to obeying *God* rather than food. We need to develop a relationship with God the Father through Jesus Christ. That is the only way we can come to trust that He truly is the One who can rescue us from our troubles. Then, the next thing we know, we are falling in love with Him. We will forget our old love called food. When we give everything to Him, our true God, He takes our hearts, our souls, our minds, and our strength and multiplies them a hundred times and gives them back to us. Just as the false god robs you, the true God gives back great dividends. You give Him the rest of your sandwich; He gives you back the next smaller dress or pants size, along with many other jewels. He is a multibillionaire! You cannot outgive the one true God. Just try Him and see! He *is* the God to follow, and He will pour out blessings for you when you give yourself totally to Him.

—April 97

How I Can Do God's Will Today

~April 18

VESSELS CANNOT BE LAZY

The sluggard says, "There is a lion in the road, a fierce lion roaming the streets!" As a door turns on its hinges, so a sluggard turns on his bed. The sluggard buries his hand in the dish; he is too lazy to bring it back to his mouth.

—Proverbs 26:13–15

We cannot be lazy or lukewarm for God, or we fail to glorify Him. For example, how could a lazy bird glorify God? If the bird was created by God to fly high, then the bird should obey and soar to great heights in the sky. If a butterfly is created to migrate thousands of miles and keep the same mate, then God is glorified when it carries out the plan. A butterfly that doesn't meet its full God-given potential is not allowing God to be a good ruler over subjects who are happy to obey His command. Outsiders could wrongfully conclude that God is a dictator—someone asking for too much from His subjects, who probably don't like Him anyway. The creations of God who are lazy prevent the invisible God from becoming delightfully visible through them. They are no longer vessels for the one true God. May we all avoid laziness, and may we be diligent with the gifts God has given us so that we can portray an accurate and glorious picture of Him.

—April 99

HOW I CAN DO GOD'S WILL TODAY

_____

_____

_____

_____

_____

_____

_____

_____

_____

_____

_____

_____

_____

_____

_____

_____

_____

_____

_____

_____

_____

_____

_____

_____

_____

_____

_____

_____

_____

_____

~April 20

SEEKING THE BLESSING

See to it that no one misses the grace of God and that no bitter root grows up to cause trouble and defile many. See that no one is sexually immoral, or is godless like Esau, who for a single meal sold his inheritance rights as the oldest son. Afterward, as you know, when he wanted to inherit this blessing, he was rejected. He could bring about no change of mind, though he sought the blessing with tears.

—Hebrews 12:15–17

God is full of love. His heart beats for you ... longs for you ... waits for you ... and desires to forgive you for foolishly falling for another love on this earth. Just do not play around with and abuse His loving invitation. Esau did not begin to appreciate the blessing he had been given. When it came to choosing between his blessing and a bowl of stew, Esau went for the meal. His blessing was a once-in-a-lifetime opportunity, and he gave it up for food. Does this sound familiar?

God has given each of us a wonderful opportunity—a chance to love Him and serve Him as our one true God. We should take this invitation very seriously, for He offers it with love and grace and mercy. We should seek His blessing and treasure it, and we should be mindful to never trade it in for some temporary earthly pleasure. Appreciate and accept the invitation!

The Spirit and the bride say, "Come!" And let him who hears say, "Come!" Whoever is thirsty, let him come; and whoever wishes, let him take the free gift of the water of life.

—Revelation 22:17

—April 27

HOW I CAN DO GOD'S WILL TODAY

April 22

PASSING DOWN OUR IDOLS

"You shall not make for yourself an idol in the form of anything in heaven above or on the earth beneath or in the waters below. You shall not bow down to them or worship them; for I, the LORD your God, am a jealous God, punishing the children for the sin of the fathers to the third and fourth generation of those who hate me, but showing love to a thousand generations of those who love me and keep my command-ments."

—Exodus 20:4–6

We pass down our idols to our children, even through the fourth generation. This includes our false idol of food. America's children have never been so large, and everyone keeps blaming it on sedentary lifestyles and fast food. But you and I know the true reason—the reason that reaches down into the hearts of our children. We have *passed down* what we adore—the food—to the next generation. Yes, our children love us so much that they will try to please us by enjoying and loving what we (the parents) love. If they see you excited about food, they will get excited to please you. If you worship academics, they will try to please you with grades. If you worship money, they will try to please you by making money, and if they don't make money, they will know down deep that they were failures in your eyes. But if you adore Christ, they will adore Christ. They know what you are surrendering to.

—April 23

HOW I CAN DO GOD'S WILL TODAY

_____

_____

_____

_____

_____

_____

_____

_____

_____

_____

_____

_____

_____

_____

_____

_____

_____

_____

_____

_____

_____

_____

_____

_____

_____

_____

_____

_____

_____

_____

April 24

GOD DISCIPLINES HIS CHILDREN

"My son, do not make light of the Lord's discipline, and do not lose heart when he rebukes you, because the Lord disciplines those he loves, and he punishes everyone he accepts as a son." Endure hardship as discipline; God is treating you as sons. For what son is not disciplined by his father? If you are not disciplined (and everyone undergoes discipline), then you are illegitimate children and not true sons. Moreover, we have all had human fathers who disciplined us and we respected them for it. How much more should we submit to the Father of our spirits and live! Our fathers disciplined us for a little while as they thought best; but God disciplines us for our good, that we may share in his holiness. No discipline seems pleasant at the time, but painful. Later on, however, it produces a harvest of righteousness and peace for those who have been trained by it.

—Hebrews 12:5b–11

As you are traveling through the hot desert of testing, think about this for a moment: Who invests more time in you than God? If you could only see the complete love of someone who takes the time to set up detailed testing, disciplining, and ways of escape just for you! What parent or teacher or friend has ever given you so much personal attention and tutoring? Who else has ever spent so much time trying to guide you, teach you, and mold you according to His heart? Who else has sent His Son to die for you? No one. Only God loves you that much.

We should welcome testing, discipline, and even punishment, for a Father who loves His children must punish them from time to time. So, my friend, do not despise it. You are a chosen son or daughter, and the result is a harvest of righteousness!

~April 25

How I Can Do God's Will Today

April 26

EXERCISING YOUR
SPIRITUAL MUSCLES

For physical training is of some value, but godliness has value for all things, holding promise for both the present life and the life to come.

— 1 Timothy 4:8

Physical exercise can be great for the body, but remember that training the *heart* in love and righteousness will help you right now *and* in eternity. You can strengthen your physical body here on earth, but you cannot take your physical body with you into heaven. However, strengthening your spiritual body—your heart, your mind, and your soul—will be your key to entering heaven! Paul wrote in 1 Timothy that physical training is of some value, but he also wrote that we should train ourselves to be godly. Do not invest more time and energy in your physical muscles than you do your *spiritual* muscles.

April 27

How I Can Do God's Will Today

_____

April 28

You Can Be Done with Sin

Therefore, since Christ suffered in his body, arm yourselves also with the same attitude, because he who has suffered in his body is done with sin. As a result, he does not live the rest of his earthly life for evil human desires, but rather for the will of God.

— 1 Peter 4:1–2

Peter, who had failed Christ at one time, held the keys to the kingdom when he wrote the words of the opening verses. Just as there were early skeptics who thought pioneer aviators could not overcome the earth's gravity, skeptics today do not believe that you can be done with sin, even though this scripture tells you that you can. The skeptics say that you are wasting your time, you are arrogant, and you are dreaming. When you fall down, they gloat and mock, saying, "What is the matter? I thought you could overcome sin." Skeptics are inside *and* outside the church building; some even live with you. They say, "Once an alcoholic, always an alcoholic," or "Once you become obese, you will just have to 'watch it' for the rest of your life."

Reread Peter's statement. Is this not one of the most exciting things you have ever read? I have broken free of the refrigerator's magnetism, and it no longer exerts a gravitational pull on me. I am flying, and you can, too. Let's imitate the pioneer pilots who reached their goals by setting their minds on what was *not* seen (their dreams of flying) rather than on what *was* seen (their skeptics and the early, inevitable failures). Sin is a rebellious attitude that does not want to submit. You have everything you need to turn it around and be *done with sin!*

~April 21

How I Can Do God's Will Today

April 30

GOD SHOOK THE EARTH

"Obey these instructions as a lasting ordinance for you and your descendants. When you enter the land that the LORD will give you as he promised, observe this ceremony. And when your children ask you, 'What does this ceremony mean to you?' then tell them, 'It is the Passover sacrifice to the LORD, who passed over the houses of the Israelites in Egypt and spared our homes when he struck down the Egyptians.'" Then the people bowed down and worshiped. The Israelites did just what the LORD commanded Moses and Aaron.

—Exodus 12:24–28

God made all of Egypt experience the terrifying plagues. Through the wind and the rain, lightning and hail, through a river of blood, insects and supernatural power, and even death itself, Satan and all the world saw that God and God alone was the One to worship, for He displayed superior power. He displayed His superior intellect, His appointment as the God of creation and as the King of kings, and His rightful position as the one true God of the universe. God commanded that this story be told from generation to generation because the message is foundational. God is indeed alive and is indeed the magnificent force creating and controlling the elements of the earth. He shook the earth to release the hold that the world had on the heart of man. He showed all nations that He was more powerful than the earth and its hold. Mankind would never again have to worry about whether the world of food and other secret loves have more power than the God of the universe. God has all the power!

May 7

How I Can Do God's Will Today

May 2

Do Not Grow Weary

Therefore, since we are surrounded by such a great cloud of witnesses, let us throw off everything that hinders and the sin that so easily entangles, and let us run with perseverance the race marked out for us. Let us fix our eyes on Jesus, the author and perfecter of our faith, who for the joy set before him endured the cross, scorning its shame, and sat down at the right hand of the throne of God. Consider him who endured such opposition from sinful men, so that you will not grow weary and lose heart. In your struggle against sin, you have not yet resisted to the point of shedding your blood.

—Hebrews 12:1–4

When you become discouraged and feel all alone, practice this: imagine a whole room filled with all the great men and women of faith. Think of everyone who has been passionate for God and would do anything to please Him! Fix your eyes on Jesus, who knew the joy that was to come and therefore endured terrible things to show the power of the Father. Why should we be discouraged or feel alone? The men and women of great faith did much more than we do, and they were required to endure greater hardships because of their faith, yet they never took their eyes and their hearts from the Father. Their actions should put a smile on your face as you think about how much they loved God. Try today to see the joy that is to come, so that you will not grow weary and lose heart!

May 3

HOW I CAN DO GOD'S WILL TODAY

May 4

THE FEAR OF MAN

Fear of man will prove to be a snare, but whoever trusts in the LORD is kept safe.

—*Proverbs 29:25*

One problem I have seen frequently that I believe is grievous to the Father is that we fear our family's rejection more than His. We put other people (especially our family members) above God in our hearts, and it shows. Where are the Abrahams who would willingly put a knife up to Isaac after God requested it? Even Jesus could not get much support from His family as He carried out His ministry and the will of the Father. His brothers taunted Him, and Joseph seemed nowhere to be found. Why do we seek man's approval over our Father's approval? If you will just stop seeking this approval from other people and look to the Lord for approval instead, you will feel such a release! God will be able to see that He is truly the One whose opinion you most care about. Once He trusts in this and finds you worthy of Him, He just might give you the approval—and even the honor—you desire from your family members.

May 5

HOW I CAN DO GOD'S WILL TODAY

May 6

LET YOUR SOUL YEARN

How lovely is your dwelling place, O LORD Almighty! My soul yearns, even faints, for the courts of the LORD; my heart and my flesh cry out for the living God.

—Psalm 84:1–2

Make sure that your soul longs for God and not for your past and secret loves. Do you remember all the loving concern and attention that you used to give to food? Can you recall how your heart used to long for all those foods that were forbidden on your latest diet? Do you remember how your heart and flesh seemed to cry out to be healthy and to be rid of the excess weight? Now, give *all* of this to God. Give your attention and concern to God and to His kingdom and His children. Let Him be the One you truly love, and let your soul long for His approval. Respond as your heart and flesh cry out for His perfect guidance and for the contentment that comes from obedience. The Lord's dwelling place has so much more to offer than the pantry! May your flesh cry out for the living God and not for the stupid food.

May 7

How I Can Do God's Will Today

May 8

EXPERIENCING *JUST ENOUGH*

The rabble with them began to crave other food, and again the Israelites started wailing and said, "If only we had meat to eat! We remember the fish we ate in Egypt at no cost—also the cucumbers, melons, leeks, onions and garlic. But now we have lost our appetite; we never see anything but this manna!" . . . Moses heard the people of every family wailing, each at the entrance to his tent. The LORD became exceedingly angry, and Moses was troubled.

—Numbers 11:4–6, 10

I would like to take a moment and point out that God's manna diet did not include all the food groups—it was a diet of bread provided by heaven. Yes, God gave them just bread and water to live on. A portion of the desert journey is learning the definition of *just enough* so that you can see how little it takes to live. How can you appreciate extra if you do not know the definition of *enough*? You may never have allowed your body to experience *just enough*. You are always gathering more manna than you need. God got very angry at His children for trying to stop His decision for them to experience *just enough*. We need to experience *just enough* financially, relationally, physiologically, and spiritually. Sometimes, even His involvement or His relationship with us is *just enough* so that we can appreciate a deeper relationship with Him. When you develop it, you will then cherish it and care for it and nurture it with all your heart. A relationship with God is *everything*. Guard it with your life!

May 9

How I Can Do God's Will Today

May 10

RUSH TOWARD THE GIANT

David said to the Philistine, "You come against me with sword and spear and javelin, but I come against you in the name of the LORD Almighty, the God of the armies of Israel, whom you have defied. This day the LORD will hand you over to me, and I'll strike you down and cut off your head. Today I will give the carcasses of the Philistine army to the birds of the air and the beasts of the earth, and the whole world will know that there is a God in Israel. All those gathered here will know that it is not by sword or spear that the LORD saves; for the battle is the LORD's, and he will give all of you into our hands." As the Philistine moved closer to attack him, David ran quickly toward the battle line to meet him.

— 1 Samuel 17:45–48

The boy David defied anyone who opposed God or God's people, including a giant Philistine who struck fear in all those who faced him. In his lifetime, David would take stones, slings, and swords against more than a few people who were antagonistic toward the glorious and perfect King of the universe. Even though David was a very successful warrior for the Lord, he made sure that all witnesses knew that every battle victory was the Lord's. David used the strength God gave him, and humbled before the power of the Lord, he always gave praise to the Father. Today, prepare your stones and sling, and if God calls, rush toward the giant, and watch how the enemies of God will fall before His power.

May 11

How I Can Do God's Will Today

May 7R

SEARCHING FOR
THE HEART OF GOD

Oh, how I love your law! I meditate on it all day long. Your commands make me wiser than my enemies, for they are ever with me. I have more insight than all my teachers, for I meditate on your statutes. I have more understanding than the elders, for I obey your precepts . . . I call out to you; save me and I will keep your statutes. I rise before dawn and cry for help; I have put my hope in your word. My eyes stay open through the watches of the night, that I may meditate on your promises.

—Psalm 119:97–100, 146–148

We have all traveled on a long spiritual journey—parallel to that of the Israelites—to get to the point where we are. We have had an Exodus from our slavery and strongholds. By now, we have tasted the heavy testing of the desert, and we have gotten the idea or we are stuck up to our necks in some sandpit. This desert is no ordinary testing. It is very heavy . . . and I know your pain. God gives us only what we can bear, and He knows the pain. The desert has been so hard for me, but I feel as if I am past some of the heavy testing. If I had to give you one piece of advice from my suffering, I would tell you this: hang on to the Word of God. I am afraid to let the Bible get far from my side. Oh, the hours I have spent searching for the heart of God, sneaking into it as if it were a box of chocolates or opening it as if it were a bank vault with a million dollars in it. My heart gets excited at the chance to sit down and see what the Father is going to tell me. I meditate on it all day long.

May 13

How I Can Do God's Will Today

_____
_____
_____
_____
_____
_____
_____
_____
_____
_____
_____
_____
_____
_____
_____
_____
_____
_____
_____
_____
_____
_____
_____
_____
_____
_____
_____
_____

May 14

THE DEPTH OF GOD'S PAIN

Oh, the depth of the riches of the wisdom and knowledge of God! How unsearchable his judgments, and his paths beyond tracing out!

— *Romans 11:33*

The LORD was grieved that he had made man on the earth, and his heart was filled with pain.

— *Genesis 6:6*

Everything about God reaches far beyond what we are capable of understanding. His wisdom, His knowledge, His decisions, His actions, His heart, His love—we cannot comprehend the depth of God's character. Have you ever thought about how big God's heart is? His heart is large enough to love every person on earth as His child. But the sad thing is that the bigger the heart of love, the greater the pain when that love is rejected. We have caused Him that kind of pain, for we reject His love daily. In fact, we have caused Him so *much* pain that He has become angry with us, even to the point that He grieved over creating us, just as it says in Genesis 6:6. Yet God blesses us with His grace and mercy. If we turn around now and give Him all of our love and devotion, which are rightfully His, He will forgive us for the pain we have caused, and His arms will take us in through Jesus' sacrifice.

May 15

How I Can Do God's Will Today

May 16

EVERYTHING PROCLAIMS
HIS GLORY

The heavens declare the glory of God; the skies proclaim the work of his hands. Day after day they pour forth speech; night after night they display knowledge. There is no speech or language where their voice is not heard. Their voice goes out into all the earth, their words to the ends of the world. In the heavens he has pitched a tent for the sun.

—Psalm 19:1–4

God speaks to us first one way and then another, according to the book of Job. I can learn something about God in everything in creation. Even "man-made" objects are the work of God's hand, and everything that has been invented or created or discovered proclaims His glory. His personality is clear to me in music too. When someone plays an instrument, I see only God, both in the creation of the instrument and in the talent of the performer. God can sing from bass to soprano, and He is a virtuoso on any instrument. The personality of God is very clear to me now, but I have much more to learn! Contemplation makes your knees and heart bow before Him. And when you truly bow before Him, you *cannot* bow down to your idols, because we *cannot* have two masters (Matthew 6:24).

How I Can Do God's Will Today

May 18

PASSION FOR GOD

As the deer pants for streams of water, so my soul pants for you,
O God.

—Psalm 42:1

You may feel that you are not emotional toward anything at all or that you don't have the passion that the psalmist had for God. But think about this in the area of food. If I were to lock you up in a room that had no food in it, you might start off asking politely for something to eat. A while later, you would ask a little more forcefully. As time went on, you might resort to begging and bribing. Eventually you would be threatening, yelling, and screaming at me to let you out or to bring some food in. Some people might threaten my life if I didn't get them some food. Have you broken into a buffet line or jumped out of the car to get ahead of the next group of people going into the same restaurant? I have known of grown men who stole money from their children's piggy banks to sneak away and feed their obsessive greed for food.

So now, have you been passionate about food? Probably. This is true for any stronghold. You are emotional after all—and this is as it should be. Now transfer the emotion and passion to God.

How I Can Do God's Will Today

May 20

WISDOM FROM ABOVE

Who is wise and understanding among you? Let him show it by his good life, by deeds done in the humility that comes from wisdom. But if you harbor bitter envy and selfish ambition in your hearts, do not boast about it or deny the truth. Such "wisdom" does not come down from heaven but is earthly, unspiritual, of the devil.

—James 3:13–15

Never blame God or Satan when you fall into temptation. The book of James sets the record straight. We are tempted by our very own evil desire, by bitter envy and selfish ambition in our hearts. If we truly trusted God, would we ever have envy or selfish ambition in our hearts? Of course not. As James stated, we would be humble, wise, and understanding, and our lives would show it. Ask God to unveil any selfish ambition in your heart, and ask Him to help you let go of it before it leads you to sin. Keep your heart and mind focused on God, and let Him take care of your life. That is wisdom from above.

May 21

HOW I CAN DO GOD'S WILL TODAY

_____

_____

_____

_____

_____

_____

_____

_____

_____

_____

_____

_____

_____

_____

_____

_____

_____

_____

_____

_____

_____

_____

_____

_____

_____

_____

_____

_____

_____

May 22

ARE YOU BUSY
OR MERELY A BUSYBODY?

*In the name of the Lord Jesus Christ, we command you, brothers, to
keep away from every brother who is idle and does not live according to
the teaching you received from us. For you yourselves know how you
ought to follow our example. We were not idle when we were with you,
nor did we eat anyone's food without paying for it. On the contrary, we
worked night and day, laboring and toiling so that we would not be a
burden to any of you. We did this, not because we do not have the right
to such help, but in order to make ourselves a model for you to follow.
For even when we were with you, we gave you this rule: "If a man will
not work, he shall not eat." We hear that some among you are idle.
They are not busy; they are busybodies. Such people we command and
urge in the Lord Jesus Christ to settle down and earn the bread they eat.
And as for you, brothers, never tire of doing what is right.*

—2 Thessalonians 3:6–13

Time is a precious commodity. It is strange how we always want
more of it, and yet I have seen too much idle time result in
nothing but trouble. People with too much time on their hands may
look busy, but they are not really busy—they are busybodies pump-
ing people for information and getting too involved in the lives of
other people. These people should be going to God for information
instead of going to the sidewalk to gather the latest gossip. And if
God doesn't give the information they are curious about, then it is
none of their concern to start with. They should instead be spending
their idle time working . . . working to earn their bread and working
to further God's kingdom. The Bible says to stay away from every
brother who is idle!

May 23

How I Can Do God's Will Today

May 24

SEEKING HIM FOR WHO HE IS

He had no beauty or majesty to attract us to him, nothing in his appearance that we should desire him.

—Isaiah 53:2b

Therefore we do not lose heart. Though outwardly we are wasting away, yet inwardly we are being renewed day by day. For our light and momentary troubles are achieving for us an eternal glory that far outweighs them all. So we fix our eyes not on what is seen, but on what is unseen. For what is seen is temporary, but what is unseen is eternal.

—2 Corinthians 4:16–18

When you are more interested in losing weight than getting close to God, you will really struggle in your desert walk. The basic obstacle here is a lack of faith. God has programmed you with the desire to lose weight, but if you want the reward of God (the weight loss) without really having to *deal* with God (submission, obedience), then that is comparable to marrying someone for money or looks instead of the purpose of being a mutual helpmate. It is completely self-serving. If you knew God better, you would understand that He would give you everything you want when you truly seek a God, Lord, Master instead of a robot, slave, or servant from the heavenlies. Yet He is clear that He is not a horrible or self-serving dictator. This is the age-old problem. God has tried to eliminate that question by remaining invisible and sending His Son to earth in a manger, even giving Him a servant role. What we need to do is to experience enough of His personality and ability that we fall in love with *Him,* and not with His things. Love Him for showing Himself as a Father, Husband, Defender, Friend, Counselor, Prince of Peace. We can serve this God. But remember that He is your God—not the other way around. You cannot keep telling God how much you are going to eat each day!

May 25

How I Can Do God's Will Today

May 26

SET APART

So he [Moses] stood at the entrance to the camp and said, "Whoever is for the LORD, come to me." And all the Levites rallied to him. Then he said to them, "This is what the LORD, the God of Israel, says: 'Each man strap a sword to his side. Go back and forth through the camp from one end to the other, each killing his brother and friend and neighbor.'" The Levites did as Moses commanded, and that day about three thousand of the people died. Then Moses said, "You have been set apart to the LORD today, for you were against your own sons and brothers, and he has blessed you this day."

—Exodus 32:26–29

The Levites were set apart from that day forward to work in the house of the Lord because they showed that they loved God more than their own families. Once again, God had found people who had the heart of Abraham, who would hold a knife up to his very own Isaac.

A great purging of drastic measure took place that day to get through to the remaining living souls. A remnant of wholly devoted souls rose to the top that day. There was hope. A heart that could house a spirit of love, healthy fear, and trust for the Father was found in the Levites. And they would be the ones who would take care of the house of the Lord from that day forward. Throughout history, God has always set apart a group of people who *wanted* Him to rule. It is the same today. We are the called out, the *ekklesia*, the church, set apart to be a holy priesthood that is totally devoted to the house of the Lord—the people of God. What an honor to be *alive*, much less to be employed by the best Boss and CEO in the universe!

May 27

How I Can Do God's Will Today

May 28

Just Say "No"
to Your Strongholds

For the grace of God that brings salvation has appeared to all men. It teaches us to say "No" to ungodliness and worldly passions, and to live self-controlled, upright and godly lives in this present age, while we wait for the blessed hope—the glorious appearing of our great God and Savior, Jesus Christ.

—*Titus 2:11–13*

Are we living self-controlled, upright, and godly lives today? Too many of us are not. We are saying "Yes" to ungodliness and worldly passions. We might find it easy to say "No" to some things, such as murder and theft, but when it comes to the everyday things that tempt us, such as extra food and the praise of men, we say, "Well ...maybe," or "Yes!" But read the Titus passage again. It does not state that the grace of God teaches us to turn down a *little* ungodliness or *some* worldly passions. No ... we must strive to be as self-controlled and upright as possible. We must say "No" to our strongholds today!

May 21

How I Can Do God's Will Today

May 30

LET GOD FILL YOUR HEART

You have filled my heart with greater joy than when their grain and new wine abound.

—Psalm 4:7

Sin is rebellion to God, and it starts in the heart. God weighs the motives of the heart, and He knows what fills your heart. There is nothing wrong with things on earth, but if you *worship* these things, you will feel drained, lethargic, worn out, and emotionless. You will not have the energy to love your spouse, children, or friends. Your heart will remain empty because you never obtain what you are seeking.

God will never let your false gods fill you up. However, people continue to try; they have put their hearts into football and basketball, computers and cars, clothes and social climbing, chocolate and desserts, children and careers. Name it, and it can be adored to a fault—to a point of worship. But if you throw yourself into worshiping God, submitting to Him, and obeying Him, then He will guide your actions. They will be rewarding, not draining. Your energy level will rise. Your heart will be filled with great joy—so much better than false idols could ever provide.

May 31

How I Can Do God's Will Today

June 1

"I Love the Father"

"But the world must learn that I love the Father and that I do exactly what my Father has commanded me."

—John 14:31a

The Bible is full of stories about people who based their lives on having a passion for God: Noah, Abraham, Moses, David, John the Baptist, Jesus. We must learn from all of these people—especially from Jesus—whom God set before us. All of these people had one thing in common—they loved God above all things. They trusted in God's judgment and guidance. They were wholehearted and passionate, and they loved obeying everything that God asked, because He was their Hero! Each of us should love the Father in the same way. When we do, serving Him is a pleasure and a privilege. Jesus said that He *loved* the Father, and He would do anything the Father asked. What a passion! Was it hard? Was there suffering involved? The answer is "Yes." However, after the suffering, the reward is more than anticipated or imagined, and this makes you trust and love the Father even more.

June R

How I Can Do God's Will Today

June 3

HAVE FAITH IN GOD'S LOVE

Observe the commands of the LORD your God, walking in his ways and revering him. For the LORD your God is bringing you into a good land—a land with streams and pools of water, with springs flowing in the valleys and hills; a land with wheat and barley, vines and fig trees, pomegranates, olive oil and honey; a land where bread will not be scarce and you will lack nothing; a land where the rocks are iron and you can dig copper out of the hills.

—Deuteronomy 8:6–9

In everything that he undertook in the service of God's temple and in obedience to the law and the commands, he sought his God and worked wholeheartedly. And so he prospered.

—2 Chronicles 31:21

People who seek and obey God can expect to be blessed and to prosper. There is nothing more fun than looking for the attention and personal love of the Father. There are so many ways that He shows us His love every day. Because I have faith in His love for me and I know He will take care of me, it is my desire to seek His will for my life. I love to do something His way and imagine that He is winking back at me. Spend each day looking for evidence of His love for you. Look for His heart and His personality in everything, and you will be rewarded. Every year with God, my life gets fuller and fuller—way beyond what I deserve. Sometimes I feel as if my heart will burst with happiness! Please know that I have my struggles—real death-to-self struggles. I just run to the refuge of the strong tower of God and wait for the sun to reappear from behind the clouds.

June 4

How I Can Do God's Will Today

June 5

His Mighty Rescue

Now the length of time the Israelite people lived in Egypt was 430 years. At the end of the 430 years, to the very day, all the LORD's divisions left Egypt. Because the LORD kept vigil that night to bring them out of Egypt, on this night all the Israelites are to keep vigil to honor the LORD for the generations to come.

—Exodus 12:40–42

If you study the plagues, you will see that they are really battles between God and Egypt—battles for our hearts. We learn from the plagues that although God has made Himself invisible, analogous to tying His right hand behind His back in a fight, He was still able to definitively beat the competition to an unrecognizable pulp. God has done *His* homework. He has shown us His passionate, jealous love, and He has shown us that He is not going to sit still and let the competition steal our hearts away. God has shown us that He is going to rescue and save us, and that He will make a distinction between those who have a heart for Him and those who have a heart for Egypt. God's awesome massacre showed that He was the God of all gods. The Israelites' hearts were drawn to follow this mighty Warrior to the desert, and ours should be too! We should follow Him and give Him honor for all generations.

June 6

HOW I CAN DO GOD'S WILL TODAY

June 7

GOD CAN FILL
YOUR EMPTY HEART

Hear, O my people, and I will warn you—if you would but listen to me, O Israel! You shall have no foreign god among you; you shall not bow down to an alien god. I am the LORD your God, who brought you up out of Egypt. Open wide your mouth and I will fill it.

—Psalm 81:8–10

We should no longer use chocolate cake to fill an empty heart! God tells us, "Open wide your mouth and I will fill it!" Open your heart to God and let Him fill you up, and this feeling you are searching for will be perfectly fulfilled. That chocolate cake will never give back to you—it only takes. But God always gives back! The next time you are tempted to pick up that fork to fill your empty heart, go to God, ask for help, and ask Him to fill you up better than the world can. I have found out that He loves the challenge, and He loves to show off! After all, He has so much to give. Your job is to open wide your heart—let your pride go and open wide your heart. You are *not* to fill it. *His* job is to *fill* it!

June 8

How I Can Do God's Will Today

June 9

THE HUMBLE ARE EXALTED

"Two men went up to the temple to pray, one a Pharisee and the other a tax collector. The Pharisee stood up and prayed about himself: 'God, I thank you that I am not like other men—robbers, evildoers, adulterers—or even like this tax collector. I fast twice a week and give a tenth of all I get.' But the tax collector stood at a distance. He would not even look up to heaven, but beat his breast and said, 'God, have mercy on me, a sinner.' I tell you that this man, rather than the other, went home justified before God. For everyone who exalts himself will be humbled, and he who humbles himself will be exalted."

—Luke 18:10–14

In this parable, Jesus said that the humble tax collector was the one who went home justified before God. He said that everyone who humbles himself will be exalted, but those who exalt themselves will be humbled. With whom do you identify—the tax collector or the Pharisee? There is something foundational about the truth of who you are and who God is. The Pharisee was wrong about both. There is nothing more irritating than a prideful person because that person just doesn't get it. The prideful person does not see that God is everything and what He says *goes*; He is the Boss. The Pharisee was self-righteous. In other words, he made the rules and he met his own rules—he was "self-right." It is similar to creating your own school and awarding yourself a Ph.D. It is so *absurd!* We need to find God's words or rules, then meet those and tremble at His leading. That is true righteousness. There's a big difference—as far apart as the tax collector and the Pharisee. Those who do not trump God's rules—such as hunger and fullness—are humble. They are afraid *not* to obey.

"This is the one I esteem: he who is humble and contrite in spirit, and trembles at my word."

—Isaiah 66:2b

June 10

HOW I CAN DO GOD'S WILL TODAY

June 11

FREE TO LOVE GOD

Then the LORD said to Moses, "Stretch out your hand over the sea so that the waters may flow back over the Egyptians and their chariots and horsemen." Moses stretched out his hand over the sea, and at daybreak the sea went back to its place. The Egyptians were fleeing toward it, and the LORD swept them into the sea. The water flowed back and covered the chariots and horsemen—the entire army of Pharaoh that had followed the Israelites into the sea. Not one of them survived.

—Exodus 14:26–28

After the Israelites passed to the other side of the Red Sea by God's mighty hand, much singing and dancing occurred. The Egyptians who pursued the Israelites were found lying dead on the seashore. God no longer allowed the Egyptians to have control over His beloved children. In the same way, food or any other stronghold no longer has control over you. Look at the ruins of Egypt. That civilization has been cursed and has never returned to its former glory as a world power. Only the lies of Satan make you think that a pan of brownies still has control over you. The truth is that you do not have to obey food anymore—you are free to love God and obey Him! I truly believe that we are the most blessed beings alive today to be able to get this chance to be devoted to God, employed by God, children of God. It is humbling and exciting.

—June JR

HOW I CAN DO GOD'S WILL TODAY

June 13

No Secret Agendas

by Michael Shamblin

"I the LORD search the heart and examine the mind...."
                                          —*Jeremiah 17:10a*

Do not think that you can conceal your hidden motives and secret agendas from God. Trying to hide your heart from God is impossible! He created us, inside and outside, and He searches our hearts and our minds. He is the only One who truly knows *who* and *what* we are deep down. Do not try to hide your thoughts from the Lord; instead, freely share your thoughts, desires, and agendas with Him. Instead of thinking that you can fool the Almighty God, try to please Him by asking Him to lead your thoughts and by doing His will. Give your heart to the Father, and watch what He can do in your life!

"But blessed is the man who trusts in the LORD, whose confidence is in him. He will be like a tree planted by the water that sends out its roots by the stream. It does not fear when heat comes; its leaves are always green. It has no worries in a year of drought and never fails to bear fruit." The heart is deceitful above all things and beyond cure. Who can understand it? "I the LORD search the heart and examine the mind, to reward a man according to his conduct, according to what his deeds deserve."
                                          —*Jeremiah 17:7–10*

June 14

How I Can Do God's Will Today

June 15

WHAT DOES GOD'S FACE LOOK LIKE?

One thing I ask of the LORD, this is what I seek: that I may dwell in the house of the LORD all the days of my life, to gaze upon the beauty of the LORD and to seek him in his temple. For in the day of trouble he will keep me safe in his dwelling; he will hide me in the shelter of his tabernacle and set me high upon a rock. Then my head will be exalted above the enemies who surround me; at his tabernacle will I sacrifice with shouts of joy; I will sing and make music to the LORD. Hear my voice when I call, O LORD, be merciful to me and answer me. My heart says of you, "Seek his face!" Your face, LORD, I will seek.

—Psalm 27:4–8

God will hear your music and your shouts of joy if you seek His face with all your heart. This means that you must seek God's face in everything you do. You need to see if He is smiling at what you are doing or if He is frowning at what you are thinking or doing. Remember that God sees *inside* our hearts and our minds. He will have an opinion about everything we consider. We should always look to Him with all our thoughts to seek His guidance first. Sometimes, when I know God sees the love I have for Him in my heart, or when I know He hears me defending His kingdom, I feel as if I can see God winking at me. I really do believe God danced the day I was born, just as He danced the day *you* were born. Seek His face because that is all that matters! If you have lived for the Lord, you know the face you will finally see will have a smile on it ... and your heart will melt.

June 16

How I Can Do God's Will Today

_____

How to Put Strongholds on the Back Burner

"'Return, faithless Israel,' declares the LORD, 'I will frown on you no longer, for I am merciful,' declares the LORD, 'I will not be angry forever. Only acknowledge your guilt—you have rebelled against the LORD your God, you have scattered your favors to foreign gods under every spreading tree, and have not obeyed me,' declares the Lord. 'Return, faithless people,' declares the LORD, 'for I am your husband.'"

—Jeremiah 3:12b–14a

Be assured that you *can* return to God or transfer your love to God and He will frown on you no longer. Even if you have developed a heart-pounding crush on food—you dress in stretch clothes for food, you plan secret rendezvous with food late at night, you hear the voice of the one you love, and thinking about food gets you out of bed in the morning—moving from Egypt to the desert is as easy as when you had a crush on some guy or girl in high school. You *loved* that person, but when the *new* guy or girl walked in, you didn't even want the old one to call your name. You didn't want the old one to write you notes or phone you, and you avoided walking down the hallway where the old one's locker was.

The old love became repulsive—and that's how it is with food for me now. I don't want my old love, food, to call my name unless I'm hungry. The good news is that your heart was made to turn around and return to God, and the tool to do this is called "choice." If I ever feel my heart beginning to wander, I find something God has made, such as flowers, and I marvel at Him all over again. When you choose today whom you will serve—our awesome Father—and focus on Him, your heart will follow. It's automatic. And you will find your heart and mind back on the Father, where they belong.

June 18

How I Can Do God's Will Today

June 11

SETTING OUR HEARTS

Since, then, you have been raised with Christ, set your hearts on things above, where Christ is seated at the right hand of God. Set your minds on things above, not on earthly things. For you died, and your life is now hidden with Christ in God. When Christ, who is your life, appears, then you also will appear with him in glory.

—Colossians 3:1–4

L isten to that again: Set your hearts and minds on things above, where Christ is seated. You know, we set a lot of things in our lives. Think about it. We set the alarm clock, and we set the timer on the oven. We set the radio, and we set the television for a favorite channel. We mark our paths to work, and we set the dates for our vacations. We set our VCRs to tape when we are gone, and we set our coffeemakers to brew coffee before we wake up.

Yes, we spend a lot of our time and energy setting things. But how much time and energy do we spend setting our hearts and our minds on Jesus Christ, our very best Advocate to the Father and the One who has saved us from sin? Today, let the oven timer and VCR and radio wait. Before you set anything else, set your heart and your mind on things above. And fix your eyes on the suffering, humble, obedient, submissive Jesus—the Author of life (Hebrews 12:2).

~ June 20

How I Can Do God's Will Today

_____

_____

_____

_____

_____

_____

_____

_____

_____

_____

_____

_____

_____

_____

_____

_____

_____

_____

_____

_____

_____

_____

_____

_____

_____

_____

_____

THE CLOUD AND THE SEA

For I do not want you to be ignorant of the fact, brothers, that our fore-
fathers were all under the cloud and that they all passed through the sea.
They were all baptized into Moses in the cloud and in the sea. They all
ate the same spiritual food and drank the same spiritual drink; for they
drank from the spiritual rock that accompanied them, and that rock was
Christ.

— 1 Corinthians 10:1–4

The cloud of God represented the presence of God. They were all baptized in this cloud and into Moses and the sea, or in other words, surrounded, covered, consecrated, and dedicated to God with the same goals and directions at the outset of the desert journey, and they all drank from the same spiritual drink—Christ. It was a drink of suffering and constant focus on the Father in the desert of life. You, too, have the goals of the Father at the outset of *your* desert journey. You have been baptized into the following of Jesus Christ, and you have realized that the only water of life available in the desert is from Him. Continue to surround yourself with Jesus Christ, and you will live and blossom in the hot desert of testing. When you are baptized, the water is in your ears, nose, eyes, and all around you. Do the same with the will of the Father. Surround yourself with His Word and will.

June 22

How I Can Do God's Will Today

_____
_____
_____
_____
_____
_____
_____
_____
_____
_____
_____
_____
_____
_____
_____
_____
_____
_____
_____
_____
_____
_____
_____
_____
_____
_____
_____
_____
_____
_____

June 23

HE CALLS US FRIENDS

"My command is this: Love each other as I have loved you. Greater love has no one than this, that he lay down his life for his friends. You are my friends if you do what I command. I no longer call you servants, because a servant does not know his master's business. Instead, I have called you friends, for everything that I learned from my Father I have made known to you. You did not choose me, but I chose you and appointed you to go and bear fruit—fruit that will last. Then the Father will give you whatever you ask in my name."

—John 15:12–16

Jesus calls us His friends. He loves us, He laid down His life for us, and He shares with us everything He has learned from God. All He tells us is that *if* we are His friends, we *will* obey what He commands. So what are His commands? First, to love Him with all our hearts, souls, minds, and strength. Then, to love our neighbor as ourselves. Does this sound as if we are going in circles? It does at times. It looks as if the genuine article—the heart that truly loves God—will, at the same time, be obedient by loving God and others. Jesus was saying, "If you love Me, it will show." *Love and obedience walk hand in hand;* in fact, you will love obeying God's commands. Think about it this way: Does a person who loves football say, "Oh, another football game is on TV. I guess I *have* to watch it"? No! He plans for it and looks forward to it and invites others to watch it with him. He *savors* it. That's the relationship you will have—a relationship where you love and the object of your affection loves you back!

June 24

How I Can Do God's Will Today

June 25

OBEDIENCE = FREEDOM,
DISOBEDIENCE = SLAVERY

Again the Israelites did evil in the eyes of the LORD. They served the Baals and the Ashtoreths, and the gods of Aram, the gods of Sidon, the gods of Moab, the gods of the Ammonites and the gods of the Philistines. And because the Israelites forsook the LORD and no longer served him, he became angry with them. He sold them into the hands of the Philistines and the Ammonites, who that year shattered and crushed them. For eighteen years they oppressed all the Israelites on the east side of the Jordan in Gilead, the land of the Amorites.

—Judges 10:6–8

Why would someone want to return to the slavery of dieting? The reason is a desire to obey self instead of God—plainly, it is disobedience to God. However, the person will blame their disobedience on *freedom*, saying, "Oh, there's too much freedom in Weigh Down†. I'm bingeing because of this new freedom to eat any food." Well, here is a major point—you cannot mix *freedom* and *disobedience*. Obedience and freedom go together, and disobedience and slavery go together. Over and over in the Old Testament, God rescued the Israelites, they again became idolatrous and disobedient, and God sent them back into slavery until He thought they had repented and could obey again.

If you want *freedom*, strive to be completely *obedient*; if you are disobedient, repent and turn immediately back to God. In other words, if you are obedient to hunger and fullness, you are free to eat anything you crave. Your focus is on obedience, and you are *free* from judgment, fat grams, scales, measuring food, calorie counting, and guilt. You're free, free, *free*! On the other hand, if you are disobedient to the amounts God has for you and the scales creep up, you will be forced into counting fat grams and watching the scales, all because you refuse to eat less food.

June 26

How I Can Do God's Will Today

June 27

ARE YOU WILLING TO BE GATHERED?

"O Jerusalem, Jerusalem, you who kill the prophets and stone those sent to you, how often I have longed to gather your children together, as a hen gathers her chicks under her wings, but you were not willing. Look, your house is left to you desolate. For I tell you, you will not see me again until you say, 'Blessed is he who comes in the name of the Lord.'"

—Matthew 23:37–39

"But your hearts must be fully committed to the LORD our God, to live by his decrees and obey his commands, as at this time."

— 1 Kings 8:61

God so adamantly opposes the heart turning away from Him that He gives us many word pictures and biblical examples to teach us never to consider this action. In Matthew, we learn how God longs to gather us to Himself, where He can protect us and provide for us. And yet we continue to turn our backs, freely giving our hearts to things on this earth that cannot protect us or give us anything in return. How insulting this must be to God! We must give our *whole* hearts to God—not just divided hearts. First Kings tells us that our hearts must be *fully* committed. It does not say that we can think about God every now and then. Let's learn from and remember all the examples and lessons God gives us in the Bible, and start today giving everything we can to Him and keeping our hearts focused on Him alone.

June 28

HOW I CAN DO GOD'S WILL TODAY

June 21

Do You Worry About God's House?

Moses was faithful as a servant in all God's house, testifying to what would be said in the future. But Christ is faithful as a son over God's house. And we are his house, if we hold on to our courage and the hope of which we boast.

—Hebrews 3:5–6

Prayer should be natural to us. In fact, I talk to God all day long. Until now, we have been very attentive to our strongholds, but now we need to reverse this. A wonderful way to direct our hearts to God is to see things from God's perspective. Have empathy for His purpose, His will, His goals. Are you concerned about how clean or decorated your house is? Well, what about *His house?* Think about all the hearts that need to be cleaned up. Are you concerned about your business? Then take time to think about *His business.* He has a hard time finding devoted employees. Worrying more about God's children than your own children is the faith that God is looking for. Are you concerned about someone's pregnancy or miscarriage? How about all the miscarriages that *God* has experienced with hearts that never beat for Him?

When I pray, my prayers reflect more interest and concern for Him than for myself; as a result, I've seen God come in and take care of my house, my business, and my children. This book is not large enough to hold the blessings that I have received because the zeal of His house consumes me. Work on this attitude, and you will fall in love with God. And remember, your heart is His house. Clean it up first!

June 30

How I Can Do God's Will Today

July 7

DEVELOP YOUR SPIRITUAL SENSES

*The LORD reigns, let the earth be glad; let the distant shores rejoice.
Clouds and thick darkness surround him; righteousness and justice are
the foundation of his throne. Fire goes before him and consumes his foes
on every side. His lightning lights up the world; the earth sees and trembles. The mountains melt like wax before the LORD, before the Lord of
all the earth. The heavens proclaim his righteousness, and all the peoples
see his glory.*

—Psalm 97:1–6

There are many people who love other people, devoting their lives
to mankind, but who do not love God. Since God is invisible, we
cannot get the usual gratification of actually hearing, touching,
smelling, tasting, and seeing Him. If we did, we would automatically
fall down in worship, since He is the best-looking, most coordinated,
and smartest—far above man and all false gods. But to keep our focus
and our priorities on God first and on man second, we must develop
our *spiritual* sight, hearing, smell, taste, and touch. Develop these spiritual senses, and taste and see that God is a genius. Your physical
senses will take a backseat to your new *spiritual* senses!

Read 2 Peter 1:3-11 to find out how you can participate in this
divine nature and be effective and productive for the Lord!

July 2

How I Can Do God's Will Today

July 3

THE STATE OF THE CHURCH

One of the seven angels who had the seven bowls full of the seven last plagues came and said to me, "Come, I will show you the bride, the wife of the Lamb."

—Revelation 21:9

The Spirit and the bride say, "Come!" And let him who hears say, "Come!" Whoever is thirsty, let him come; and whoever wishes, let him take the free gift of the water of life.

—Revelation 22:17

I hear many people claim that their six- to twelve-month plateau in weight loss is the desert. But think with me. If we call this a desert, then it is quicksand. And now we're worse off than we were before because we've labeled this delusion as a more progressive part of the journey of salvation instead of a retreat. Instead of depicting the desert as a wonderful place to grow nearer to God, we have concocted such a defeated desert scene that young sojourners would never want to follow in our footsteps.

I see this as the largest delusion of the body of Christ—an invisible, undetectable cancer permeating every denomination. Instead of a healthy, athletic, powerful, and magnetic body of Christ, we've made a sad, sickly, cancerous body of Christ lying on a hospital bed with an IV bag. We devise evangelical church programs to invite the world into this "saved" state, and yet we can't even get up and walk. This is hardly an evangelical state for the body of Christ. Who wants this? Week after week, people sit on church pews, enslaved to the world. They claim, "I'm saved! I'm saved!" and yet their necks are strangled by a ball and chain, and they wonder why they can't drink in the Water of Life and gain strength from the Bread of Life. We have been offered a free gift out of slavery; however, we must "come" and "take the free gift" out of the prison cells.

~ July 4

How I Can Do God's Will Today

July 5

THE FOUNTAIN OF LIFE

But the LORD is the true God; he is the living God, the eternal King. When he is angry, the earth trembles; the nations cannot endure his wrath. "Tell them this: 'These gods, who did not make the heavens and the earth, will perish from the earth and from under the heavens.'"

—Jeremiah 10:10–11

"My people have committed two sins: They have forsaken me, the spring of living water, and have dug their own cisterns, broken cisterns that cannot hold water."

—Jeremiah 2:13

Have we forgotten what a god is? The true God doesn't *need* anything. If He did, He wouldn't be God. Jehovah doesn't need anything you could give Him in money or time or help. He doesn't need your heart or your soul or your mind. That's why He can give it back to you, plus some. He is the Source of time, and He is the Source of love. He is the Supplier of gold, and He is the Creator of food. He is the Fountain of Life. Yes, I have experienced this truth. He is the *Alpha*, and He is the *Omega*. He is the Beginning, and He is the End. He is the *only* Source—find me another. Try giving your heart to football, baseball, basketball, or hockey. As you adore the athletes, the irony is that many times you become a couch potato and somehow full of anger. Try making your spouse a god, and you will run him or her off. Your spouse is your helpmate, not your god. Just try giving your heart to money, and you'll find yourself in poverty. Try giving yourself to sexual lust, and you'll find yourself divorced, lonely, or diseased. Find me a god—you can't. There's only One. He is the *only* true Fountain of Life. Don't try digging your own wells or cisterns—they cannot hold water.

July 6

How I Can Do God's Will Today

_____
_____
_____
_____
_____
_____
_____
_____
_____
_____
_____
_____
_____
_____
_____
_____
_____
_____
_____
_____
_____
_____
_____
_____
_____
_____
_____
_____
_____
_____
_____

July 7

SEEKING GOD FIRST

But seek [ye] first his kingdom and his righteousness, and all these things will be given to you as well.

—Matthew 6:33

Then the word of the LORD *came through the prophet Haggai: "Is it a time for you yourselves to be living in your paneled houses, while this house remains a ruin?"* . . . *"You expected much, but see, it turned out to be little. What you brought home, I blew away. Why?" declares the* LORD *Almighty. "Because of my house, which remains a ruin, while each of you is busy with his own house."*

—Haggai 1:3–4, 9

Most of our desert storms break out because we do not automatically seek God *first* as we are told to do. Most of us have come only as close as "seek ye fifth" or "seek ye sixth"; "seek ye first" is not the natural instinct it should be. Instead of trying to do things or worrying about things that are not part of your job description, practice giving your worries to God. Spend your time worrying about His kingdom—starting with your heart, then the hearts of His children. Worry about His house more than your house. Forming this habit will make a great difference in your weight loss and in every area of your life. God will come back in and do more for your children and your house than you could think or imagine.

July 8

How I Can Do God's Will Today

July 9

BE ON YOUR WATCH

He told them this parable: "Look at the fig tree and all the trees. When they sprout leaves, you can see for yourselves and know that summer is near. Even so, when you see these things happening, you know that the kingdom of God is near. I tell you the truth, this generation will certainly not pass away until all these things have happened. Heaven and earth will pass away, but my words will never pass away. Be careful, or your hearts will be weighed down with dissipation, drunkenness and the anxieties of life, and that day will close on you unexpectedly like a trap. For it will come upon all those who live on the face of the whole earth. Be always on the watch, and pray that you may be able to escape all that is about to happen, and that you may be able to stand before the Son of Man."

—Luke 21:29–36

Jesus spoke these words as a precaution to us to stay awake. We must remain aware and focused on the kingdom of God and its advancement. If we continue to focus on the worries of everyday life, the day of the Lord will appear before we realize what is happening, and it will be like being caught in a trap. In other words, focusing on this earth will only weigh us down and keep us from looking up to God in heaven. Jesus told us to be on the watch, and one day we will be able to stand before God without worry. Many people have been weighed down with frittering their lives away with drugs, drunkenness, and the anxieties of life. Please stay in the Word of God and live as one watchful and expectant of the life to come!

~July 10

HOW I CAN DO GOD'S WILL TODAY

July 11

JESUS PARTS THE IMPOSSIBLE BARRIER

Therefore, if anyone is in Christ, he is a new creation; the old has gone, the new has come! All this is from God, who reconciled us to himself through Christ and gave us the ministry of reconciliation: that God was reconciling the world to himself in Christ, not counting men's sins against them. And he has committed to us the message of reconciliation.

—2 Corinthians 5:17–19

There is no way to get from Egypt to the desert unless you find a way to cross the Red Sea. The Red Sea is a big barrier. You cannot swim across it because the currents would wash you away. In the same way, we cannot gain the opportunity to get to the heart of the Father on our own. We have all had a bad attitude toward submitting to Him as Boss. But here is the great news—the sacrifice of Jesus parts this impossible barrier and allows us to walk on dry land to the heart of our King and Boss. God reconciled the sinners to Himself in Christ. Our rebellious attitude toward our King and Boss is sin, and it sends our Boss far away from us because no boss likes enemies. Yet, according to Romans 5:10, "if, when we were God's enemies, we were reconciled to him through the death of his Son, how much more, having been reconciled, shall we be saved through his life!" Reconciliation is a changed relationship between God and man when there has existed a state of enmity. (Jesus is worthy of praise for bringing the employees and Boss back together.) Now we must understand that we have the ministry of reconciliation.

—July 12

How I Can Do God's Will Today

July 13

THE MAKER OF ALL THINGS

*The LORD God formed the man from the dust of the ground and breathed
into his nostrils the breath of life, and the man became a living being.*
—Genesis 2:7

*As you do not know the path of the wind, or how the body is formed in
a mother's womb, so you cannot understand the work of God, the
Maker of all things.*
—Ecclesiastes 11:5

We need to recognize that God is the Creator, the CEO, the
Owner, and the Boss of our bodies. Why would *we* ever want
to run a business that is not *our* business? It would be like walking
into a large department store and telling everyone there that you
were taking over. We know that would be ridiculous because you
didn't build the business, finance the business, locate the business,
purchase the merchandise, or hire the employees. *It's not your right.*
Well, the analogy is that you did not create your body, make your
organs, or teach your body parts to function together, and yet *you've*
decided that *you're* going to run this body and override *God's* decisions about how much you are going to eat and drink! I cannot
believe the grief we give our great Boss, and I cannot believe the
complaints with which we burden our Lord. Decide today that you
are going to let God run His business and that you are going to be a
willing and submissive employee to this wonderful Boss!

—July 14

HOW I CAN DO GOD'S WILL TODAY

July 15

LOOK FOR THE FRUIT

Brothers, think of what you were when you were called. Not many of you were wise by human standards; not many were influential; not many were of noble birth. But God chose the foolish things of the world to shame the wise; God chose the weak things of the world to shame the strong. He chose the lowly things of this world and the despised things—and the things that are not—to nullify the things that are, so that no one may boast before him.

—1 Corinthians 1:26–29

But avoid foolish controversies and genealogies and arguments and quarrels about the law, because these are unprofitable and useless. Warn a divisive person once, and then warn him a second time. After that, have nothing to do with him. You may be sure that such a man is warped and sinful; he is self-condemned.

—Titus 3:9–11

People often turn to those who have met the world's standards of academic excellence for the answers about how to live from day to day. Other people turn to those who have achieved the world's standards of wealth or popularity. And there are still others who do not want a simple answer, but want to have scholarly debates and arguments before settling upon answers to life's questions.

However, the Bible states that we should avoid debates and arguments, and that the wisdom of the world will be made foolish by our awesome God! It also tells us how to know whom to follow—by looking for the *fruit* of the teaching (Matthew 7:15-20). This has always been the barometer in my life: if a principle is from God, it will bear fruit. It will give you peace that is virtually free of anger, liberating you from compulsive behaviors. You will ultimately feel a deep, loving nature permeating your soul, in contrast to an unloving nature at the base of your soul. If you are looking for answers, listen to people who are focused only on doing the Lord's will.

— July 16

HOW I CAN DO GOD'S WILL TODAY

July 17

Love, Knowledge, and Obedience

Remember how the LORD your God led you all the way in the desert these forty years, to humble you and to test you in order to know what was in your heart, whether or not you would keep his commands.

—Deuteronomy 8:2

"Whoever has my commands and obeys them, he is the one who loves me. He who loves me will be loved by my Father, and I too will love him and show myself to him."

—John 14:21

We know that we have come to know him if we obey his commands. The man who says, "I know him," but does not do what he commands is a liar, and the truth is not in him. But if anyone obeys his word, God's love is truly made complete in him. This is how we know we are in him: Whoever claims to live in him must walk as Jesus did.

—1 John 2:3–6

It is so clear from these passages that obedience is a huge factor in knowing what is truly in our hearts. Jesus would try to make it as clear as possible, first saying it one way, then another. He was making sure that we got the message while He was here on earth. Obedience is the major way to measure and grow the love in our hearts for God. After all, it is how we know that our children love us, trust us, and respect us. Obedience is how employers know the hearts of employees, and patronizing obedience and false love are eventually revealed. It is tragic that the concept of obedience has become *optional* to Christians rather than *foundational*. This is wrong, for the Word teaches: "This is how we know we are in him: Whoever claims to live in him must walk as Jesus did." (1 John 2:5-6). I love obedience and submission, and I always look for more and more ways to submit, for it brings me such happiness.

July 18

How I Can Do God's Will Today

July 79

Two Deceptions

Finally, be strong in the Lord and in his mighty power. Put on the full armor of God so that you can take your stand against the devil's schemes. For our struggle is not against flesh and blood, but against the rulers, against the authorities, against the powers of this dark world and against the spiritual forces of evil in the heavenly realms.

—Ephesians 6:10–12

After years of talking with people who are trying to lay down sin in their lives, I have found two distinct deceptions that Satan whispers to God's children. The first deception is that you are doing right and are fine, when really you are *not* doing fine. The second deception comes when you *are* doing right; Satan whispers that you are *not* doing right, causing you to question yourself. When you hear these deceptive lies, the first thing you should do is get into God's Word and find out the truth. Search for it, seek it, and write it on your heart. Make sure you're not lying to yourself. If you *are* sinning, realize the truth that you cannot continue in sin. If you are *not* sinning, realize that you should have confidence before God. And be sure to stay alert because this is a continual battle! Does a soldier put on his armor just one day? No! He puts it on every day. Choose to be a soldier, and choose to start transforming your mind so that you understand who you are and what this whole battle is about.

~July 20

How I Can Do God's Will Today

July 21

THE GOD OF ALL COMFORT

A bruised reed he will not break, and a smoldering wick he will not snuff out.

—Isaiah 42:3a

Many people do not know how to comfort another human being. When my collie Virginia had puppies, raising the little balls of fur was so much fun. But I noticed that if one of them got left out of the feeding or got stuck between a table and chair or got turned around for a while, the other puppies didn't care. They didn't care about anything but their own personal needs. This is true in the animal world, and I have found it to be basically true for mankind, too. But God is totally different. Just as every child instinctively runs to his mother to display his "hurt" so she can kiss it to make it better, we can always run to the Father to help our hurt go away. God will never be more concerned over His own needs than ours, and He will never turn away from those truly seeking Him on His terms. When we come to Him for help, we will suddenly become the most important people to Him, and He will be there for us, no matter what time it is or what our need is. If you are trying to help introduce some people to this love of the Father, whether they are coworkers, friends, or family members, remember to be patient and gentle so that you do not break them or snuff out the small but growing interest in Christ they already have.

How I Can Do God's Will Today

July 23

THE TRAINABLE
HEARTS OF CHILDREN

Train a child in the way he should go, and when he is old he will not turn from it.

—*Proverbs 22:6*

All your sons will be taught by the LORD, and great will be your children's peace.

—*Isaiah 54:13*

Because the hearts of children are so trainable, we must not get in the way of God by teaching and suggesting things that confuse them. To teach your children how to eat, you must first learn how to turn them over to the Father. There are many books about how parents should raise their children, but I know better than to suggest you are the "all in all" for your children. Rather, I suggest parental information about how to be wholly devoted to the Father, and then how to get your heart right so that you can experience what I have experienced—God as the personal Tutor of your children. God's plan is uncomplicated. You don't have to be talented to be able to rejoice in having great children. It starts with *you* ... you want to get your own heart right with food (or any stronghold) because we pass our idols down from one generation to the next generation. Pursue righteousness, and the promise to you is that the Lord will teach your children.

— July 24

HOW I CAN DO GOD'S WILL TODAY

_____

_____

_____

_____

_____

_____

_____

_____

_____

_____

_____

_____

_____

_____

_____

_____

_____

_____

_____

_____

_____

_____

_____

_____

_____

_____

_____

_____

July 25

He Who Seeks, Finds

O God, you are my God, earnestly I seek you; my soul thirsts for you,
my body longs for you, in a dry and weary land where there is no water.
I have seen you in the sanctuary and beheld your power and your glory.
Because your love is better than life, my lips will glorify you. I will praise
you as long as I live, and in your name I will lift up my hands. My soul
will be satisfied as with the richest of foods; with singing lips my mouth
will praise you.

—Psalm 63:1–5

You know, the thought and smell of food used to get me out of bed in the morning. Now, thinking about God and what kind of day He is planning for me gets me out of bed. I will give all my senses over to God. I dress for Him. Although I do not see Him visibly, I can sense when He is near. I am hungry to read His Word. I ask Him to help me and guide me in everything, big and small, throughout the day. And I have found that since my senses have come alive to Him, I can recognize all the times that He answers my prayers in very personal and special ways. So many special little prayers were answered for one woman that she told me she does not call things "coincidences" anymore, but "Godincidences"! Ask God to guide your day, and pray for what you need from Him. Then, keep your senses alert and watch as He opens the door to you! To me, God's love is better than life!

July 26

HOW I CAN DO GOD'S WILL TODAY

July 27

THE LORD'S GENTLE WHISPER

The LORD said, "Go out and stand on the mountain in the presence of the LORD, for the LORD is about to pass by." Then a great and powerful wind tore the mountains apart and shattered the rocks before the LORD, but the LORD was not in the wind. After the wind there was an earthquake, but the LORD was not in the earthquake. After the earthquake came a fire, but the LORD was not in the fire. And after the fire came a gentle whisper. When Elijah heard it, he pulled his cloak over his face and went out and stood at the mouth of the cave. Then a voice said to him, "What are you doing here, Elijah?"

— 1 Kings 19:11–13

This story about Elijah demonstrates that you need to watch for the Lord very carefully. He is such a gentleman—He will not push Himself on you, so you must listen closely for His gentle whisper. Elijah heard the Lord's whisper and obeyed it. We fell in love with food this way. We listened carefully to its whisper from the pantry. We heard its small voice calling us from the refrigerator late at night, and we obeyed it. Make sure today that you tell your old boss, food, that you do not have to do anything that it says! And then, make sure you have ears and eyes only for the Lord God Almighty. Listen for His whisper today, and look and see His awesome, yet humble authority. Amazing! Intriguing! Precious!

July 28

How I Can Do God's Will Today

_July 21

THE BEAUTIFUL NIGHTS

Sing for joy to God our strength; shout aloud to the God of Jacob! Begin the music, strike the tambourine, play the melodious harp and lyre. Sound the ram's horn at the New Moon, and when the moon is full, on the day of our Feast; this is a decree for Israel, an ordinance of the God of Jacob.

—Psalm 81:1–4

Over the years, God has awakened me in the middle of the night to see the clear full moon. Every time I see it, I have appreciation in my heart for God's handiwork. I feel as if God has been robbed because full moons have often been associated with superstition and the appearance of evil spirits. The truth is quite the opposite—these beautiful nights truly belong to the Lord! There are eighteen references in the Bible to new moon and full moon celebrations among the Israelites. Today, we know that our hearts should be as devoted one day as the next, and we know that one day is not any more special than another. In other words, we should praise Him every day. We should never neglect praising God for all the variety He provides to make Himself known and to make life fun and exciting! Let's put a stop to full moons being associated with evil. Let's return the full moon to the setting where it belongs—in praise of God!

July 30

How I Can Do God's Will Today

_July 31

ARE YOU PURE IN HEART?

"Blessed are the pure in heart, for they will see God."

—*Matthew 5:8*

Some people tend to sling mud on people who are upright, righteous, or blameless. God said, "Have you considered my servant Job? There is no one on earth like him; he is blameless and upright, a man who fears God and shuns evil" (Job 1:8). The psalmist declared, "Blessed are they whose ways are blameless, who walk according to the law of the LORD. Blessed are they who keep his statutes and seek him with all their heart. They do nothing wrong; they walk in his ways" (Psalm 119:1–3). And Jesus said, "I tell you that in the same way there will be more rejoicing in heaven over one sinner who repents than over ninety-nine righteous persons who do not need to repent" (Luke 15:7). There are those who have crucified themselves and who live by the Spirit of God and will of God. And then there are those who have the arrogant "I want to do things my way" attitude or who are sinners. Paul taught us, "Brothers, if someone is caught in a sin, you who are spiritual should restore him gently. But watch yourself, or you also may be tempted" (Galatians 6:1). In other words, be careful that the "you deserve to make your own decisions for your body" attitude doesn't rub off on you!

How do you become pure in heart? Well, Peter told us, "Now that you have purified yourselves by obeying the truth ..." (1 Peter 1:22a). *Obeying the truth* is comprehensive. Stay in the Word and apply it!

~ August 7

How I Can Do God's Will Today

_____

_____

_____

_____

_____

_____

_____

_____

_____

_____

_____

_____

_____

_____

_____

_____

_____

_____

_____

_____

_____

_____

_____

_____

_____

_____

_____

_____

August 2

THE PURSUIT OF
THE FATHER FIRST

For the message of the cross is foolishness to those who are perishing, but to us who are being saved it is the power of God. For it is written: "I will destroy the wisdom of the wise; the intelligence of the intelligent I will frustrate." Where is the wise man? Where is the scholar? Where is the philosopher of this age? Has not God made foolish the wisdom of the world? For since in the wisdom of God the world through its wisdom did not know him, God was pleased through the foolishness of what was preached to save those who believe.

— 1 Corinthians 1:18–21

There is nothing wrong with pursuing academics to honor and glorify the Father, but if you are doing so only to glorify *Him*, why would you be upset at a B on a report card? Being upset with yourself or your teachers reveals that the glory was sought for *self*. Nothing is harder on a teacher than a parent-child team existing for the glory of the child. Nothing is harder on a coach than a parent-child duo striving for the glory of the child. These parents don't know the promise of the "seek ye first" lifestyle, and they encourage goals that only get the child more and more caught up in a rat race that will never satisfy. Their mistaken belief is that a "seek ye first" lifestyle is ungodly and unbalanced. "Isn't it true," they argue, "that God wants you to make it in this life?" But this lack of understanding of God's personality is dangerous. God Himself says His people *perish* from a lack of knowledge of Him (Hosea 4:6). Matthew 6:33 teaches that if you "seek *first* his kingdom and his righteousness," then "all these things will be given to you as well." Learning the true meaning of "seek ye first" gives you blessings overflowing. You can save your child from the pain of loving this earth and the emptiness of a misguided mission if you teach him to go *first* to the Father, expect all things from Him, and develop all gifts to His glory only.

August 3

How I Can Do God's Will Today

_____

_____

_____

_____

_____

_____

_____

_____

_____

_____

_____

_____

_____

_____

_____

_____

_____

_____

_____

_____

_____

_____

_____

_____

_____

_____

_____

_____

_____

_____

_____

_____

_____

 August 4

LOVE OTHERS AS YOURSELF

*After all, no one ever hated his own body, but he feeds and cares for it,
just as Christ does the church—for we are members of his body.*

—Ephesians 5:29–30

The Bible tells us that we naturally love and care for ourselves. Since this is true, we should take the actions of love that we give ourselves and give them to someone else too. As God said in Leviticus 19:18, "Love your neighbor as yourself." Show concern for others—feed them, clothe them, and care for them. Don't focus constantly on pampering yourself because it will provide only temporary delight, and you will despise your overly self-indulgent actions. Self-indulgence also turns other people off, making you even more isolated.

People of the world say that what you feel about yourself dictates whether you will have a good "eating" day. But I say getting your focus off self and onto God and obedience to Him will cause you to have a good "eating" day. If you love and trust the Lord, you will feed yourself the appropriate amount and not indulge in desire eating. You will be more in love with God for saving you from preoccupation with yourself. Since we do love ourselves, we should have a healthy, appropriate focus on care of self. But we tend to think if a little bit is good, then a lot is better. However, in the case of excessive self-love, it is empty and usually empties our pocketbooks. The balanced way leads to life; the other leads to death.

August 5

How I Can Do God's Will Today

_____
_____
_____
_____
_____
_____
_____
_____
_____
_____
_____
_____
_____
_____
_____
_____
_____
_____
_____
_____
_____
_____
_____
_____

HIS FAVOR LASTS A LIFETIME

Sing to the LORD, you saints of his; praise his holy name. For his anger lasts only a moment, but his favor lasts a lifetime; weeping may remain for a night, but rejoicing comes in the morning.

—Psalm 30:4–5

Many times I have sat in church on a Sunday evening and watched people listlessly drag themselves through the motions of their worship. These same people have red-and-white pom-poms and apply red and white paint to their faces to root for their favorite college team. They jump up after the worship service—which is sometimes a sad name for what actually took place—and rush to a basketball game for their true worship. They know the name of every team player and every statistic, and they scream, yell, cheer, and jump up and down for the players. In the same way, I have known of people who spent the whole Sunday morning worship service dreaming about the local restaurant buffet they would visit as soon as the service ended. They have memorized the menu, they have tried every item available, and they sit at a regular table at every visit.

Is there something in your life that brings out the excitement in your heart? It could be a ball game, a sale at the mall, a great buffet table, a daily soap opera, or anything at all. Each of us has a heart, and we know how to worship something. We are all worshiping something this very minute, but our hearts and our worship may be misplaced. Examine your heart today, and begin to sing to and worship only the Lord. Give devotion where it is deserved. Earthly pleasures will last only a moment, but God's favor lasts a lifetime—yes, for eternity.

~August 7

How I Can Do God's Will Today

_____

_____

_____

_____

_____

_____

_____

_____

_____

_____

_____

_____

_____

_____

_____

_____

_____

_____

_____

_____

_____

_____

_____

_____

_____

_____

_____

_____

_____

_____

_____

_____

_____

_____

_____

August 8

WALLOWING IN THE PIGPEN

"When he came to his senses, he said, 'How many of my father's hired men have food to spare, and here I am starving to death! I will set out and go back to my father and say to him: Father, I have sinned against heaven and against you. I am no longer worthy to be called your son; make me like one of your hired men.' So he got up and went to his father. But while he was still a long way off, his father saw him and was filled with compassion for him; he ran to his son, threw his arms around him and kissed him. The son said to him, 'Father, I have sinned against heaven and against you. I am no longer worthy to be called your son.' But the father said to his servants, 'Quick! Bring the best robe and put it on him. Put a ring on his finger and sandals on his feet.'"

—Luke 15:17–22

When the prodigal son got up, crawled out of the pigpen, and returned home to his father, he received the ring, the robe, and the prime rib dinner. You know, we often get angry at God for not presenting us with the ring, the robe, and the steak while we are still wallowing in the pigpen. We want Him to come to us; we don't want to humbly go to Him with contrite hearts. Repent of that attitude, and praise God that He does not reward Sodom and Gomorrah. Even more, praise God that He *does* reward those who earnestly seek Him—check out the rings, robes, and banquet tables for the sons at home with God! Check out how the Father waits for someone to finally realize that he is not a good boss, he has no continual source of money or food—only God the Father does. When we finally realize we are not gods and when we realize we are not smarter than God, we can humble ourselves and come home—*depend* on the Father— since we are *not* the Father. Check out how God puts His arms around the repentant child and kisses him. That is your God!

August 9

How I Can Do God's Will Today

_____

_____

_____

_____

_____

_____

_____

_____

_____

_____

_____

_____

_____

_____

_____

_____

_____

_____

_____

_____

_____

_____

_____

_____

_____

~August 10

ASKING, SEEKING, AND KNOCKING

"Ask and it will be given to you; seek and you will find; knock and the door will be opened to you. For everyone who asks receives; he who seeks finds; and to him who knocks, the door will be opened."

—Matthew 7:7–8

I hope that you ask and seek and knock all the time on God's door to discover His will and to bring your requests before Him. God makes the best decisions, and He knows the best gifts and how to indulge you with them. If you will just be patient and obedient, the results will blow you away! Don't be afraid that if you wait on God, you will be disappointed. To the contrary, He will surprise you beyond your wildest dreams! Ask and seek your heavenly Father, and then obey His will for your life.

Some people never ask; others *do* ask, but they ask for their own gain so that they can rule, for their own selfish ambition or pleasures. (See James 4:1–3.) What are we to ask for? Well, start with "What is my humble place on this earth?" and "Why was I created?" All the animals, fish, birds, and insects know their places. You need to seek God's will and His plan. He has a very big business to run, and you are a part of the plan. When you follow through with His plan, the result is peace and blessings for you, your family, and your future.

August 11

HOW I CAN DO GOD'S WILL TODAY

August 12

QUIT MAKING EXCUSES

The LORD does not look at the things man looks at. Man looks at the outward appearance, but the LORD looks at the heart.

—*1 Samuel 16:7b*

These days, almost everyone seems to be trying to improve his physical appearance. Although there is nothing wrong with trying to look better, people need to work on something much more important. This is the heart. Now, I am not talking about the physical heart that pumps blood, but the *spiritual* heart. In many cases, people focus on the outside of the body while they ignore the most important part of the body. We need to work on getting our hearts right before God. We need to purify our hearts so God can dwell in us and work through us. Get rid of the sin in your life and quit making excuses to God, and then the other things will fall into place.

~August 13

How I Can Do God's Will Today

August 14

OUR SPIRITUAL ACT OF WORSHIP

Therefore, I urge you, brothers, in view of God's mercy, to offer your bodies as living sacrifices, holy and pleasing to God—this is your spiritual act of worship. Do not conform any longer to the pattern of this world, but be transformed by the renewing of your mind. Then you will be able to test and approve what God's will is—his good, pleasing and perfect will.

—Romans 12:1–2

Like everyone, I have suffered in my life. But instead of dwelling on my trials and hardships, I have grown into a happy, content person because of the suffering. I feel this way because I have learned never to defy or rebel against God's desert leadings—even when it means suffering. After all, God's will was that Jesus should suffer all the way to death on the cross, and because Jesus died to His own desire (to have the cup taken from Him), He stepped forward and faced His suffering that day, saying, "not my will, but *yours* be done" (Luke 22:42). Because of that act of reverent submission and acceptance of suffering, I have received one of the greatest gifts from God that I could receive ... forgiveness and a home in heaven with Him someday. Because of the personal suffering God has placed before me and because of the way He holds my hand as I stand to face the hardships, I know God much better now. Even in the times when I don't have a clue about the specific reason for my suffering, I trust completely that God knows what He is up to. Voluntarily offer your body as a living sacrifice—holy and pleasing to God.

August 15

How I Can Do God's Will Today

_____

_____

_____

_____

_____

_____

_____

_____

_____

_____

_____

_____

_____

_____

_____

_____

_____

_____

_____

_____

_____

_____

_____

_____

_____

_____

_____

_____

_____

_____

_____

_____

_____

_____

_____

_____

~August 16

LOVE FOR GOD GROWS

Because of the increase of wickedness, the love of most will grow cold,
but he who stands firm to the end will be saved.

—Matthew 24:12–13

If you think a crush on God may go away and be replaced by a "more mature," emotionless love, think again. Your love for food grows more and more. Statistics show us that people in developed countries are becoming larger and larger and more and more passionate for their food. According to most conservative estimates, at the rate we are going, half the population will be obese in the next twenty years. Have you noticed that the older you get, the harder it is to lose weight? That's because you become increasingly attached to what you adore. So love *does* grow—for whatever you have given your heart to.

As for me, my love for *God* has grown more and more. I can't get Him out of my heart and mind. It is a passion, and that is how God wants it. Matthew 6:24 states, "No one can serve two masters." Why? Because you have only one heart, and it was made to be devoted to one master. Had the children of God stayed in Egypt, they would have become more and more enslaved. If you keep obeying food, five years from now you will be even more attached to it than you are right now. But if you start devoting your heart to God today by obeying God with hunger and fullness and not obeying food, then five years from now you will be even more attached to Him and less attached to food. The next time you see me, I will be even more deeply in love with God. How exciting!

~August 17

How I Can Do God's Will Today

_____
_____
_____
_____
_____
_____
_____
_____
_____
_____
_____
_____
_____
_____
_____
_____
_____
_____
_____
_____
_____
_____
_____
_____
_____
_____
_____
_____
_____

~August 18

Do Not Save Yourself

The people stood watching, and the rulers even sneered at him. They said, "He saved others; let him save himself if he is the Christ of God, the Chosen One." The soldiers also came up and mocked him. They offered him wine vinegar and said, "If you are the king of the Jews, save yourself." There was a written notice above him, which read: THIS IS THE KING OF THE JEWS. One of the criminals who hung there hurled insults at him: "Aren't you the Christ? Save yourself and us!"

—Luke 23:35–39

Throughout the ministry of Jesus, He was mocked, scorned, and tested. He could have saved Himself from any of these trials at any time, but He did not. Then, on the day when Jesus hung on the cross, He was tempted by others three times to save Himself from the pain and suffering He was enduring. Again, He refused. He knew it was more important to look to God. If God wanted to save Him, He would. But it was God's will that Jesus suffer so that many could be saved. We will be called to walk in the steps of Jesus—steps of suffering.

As you are feeling the hot desert testing right now, I'm sure you will be tempted to save yourself from your suffering. You may want to give yourself more food than God has decided to give you. But stop and think a minute before you do. Look to Jesus Christ for the perfect example of trusting the suffering blow from God. Do not save yourself and become your own boss and god again. Pass this test and you'll see God rewarding you. Jesus is at the right-hand side of God. You will have reward in heaven!

~*August 11*

HOW I CAN DO GOD'S WILL TODAY

_____

_____

_____

_____

_____

_____

_____

_____

_____

_____

_____

_____

_____

_____

_____

_____

_____

_____

_____

_____

_____

_____

_____

_____

_____

_____

_____

_____

~August 20

Is He Your Lord?

"You shall not misuse the name of the LORD your God, for the LORD will not hold anyone guiltless who misuses his name."

—*Exodus 20:7*

You should never call the Lord "Lord" when He is *not* the Lord of your life. Before you say, "But He *is* my Lord," consider this for a minute. If you refuse to obey His commands or if you cannot give Him your whole heart, then He is not your Lord. You can't just call Him a name such as "Lord" if you do not follow through with your heart, your mind, and your actions. If you call Him "Lord" while you are bowing down to other idols on this earth, you will confuse many people and be a stumbling block to those who are trying to figure out the relationship they should have with God. We should take His role in our lives very seriously, and we should never misuse His honorable and glorious name by calling Him "Lord" when He is not on the throne of our hearts. Many people have asked God into their hearts—but not on the *throne* of their hearts—not as the Lord, King, Master, Boss. If you are on the throne with food or anything else (How do you know? Because you are still overweight, depressed, etc.), then where do you think the God of the universe is? Under your leadership? No! His Holy Spirit is not there! Start over; go home; humble yourself and bow to God daily.

HOW I CAN DO GOD'S WILL TODAY

August 22

COME ... LET US WORSHIP HIM!

"We saw his star in the east and have come to worship him."

—Matthew 2:2b

Whom, or what, have you come to worship? Do you adore the praise of other people? Then you have missed the mark. Do you behold the food? Then you will become like a refrigerator. Do you adore money and material possessions? Then you will be greedy and alone. But ... do you behold and adore Christ? Then you will be *fulfilled.* You will become like Christ at heart, serving and worshiping the Father. Just as these men saw His star in the east and traveled a distance to worship Him, we should look for His signs, seek to be near Him, and worship Him above all things. Psalm 34:5 tells us, "Those who look to him are radiant; their faces are never covered with shame." So come ... let us worship Him!

The early Christians understood how wonderful the grace of God was that He allowed all who repented and turned toward Him, believing in Him as the one true God and Jesus as the Son of God, to become children of God—even the Gentiles. These Christians were so appropriately humbled that they met together daily to encourage one another.

They devoted themselves to the apostles' teaching and to the fellowship, to the breaking of bread and to prayer. Everyone was filled with awe, and many wonders and miraculous signs were done by the apostles. All the believers were together and had everything in common. Selling their possessions and goods, they gave to anyone as he had need. Every day they continued to meet together in the temple courts. They broke bread in their homes and ate together with glad and sincere hearts, praising God and enjoying the favor of all the people. And the Lord added to their number daily those who were being saved. —Acts 2:42-47

—August 23

How I Can Do God's Will Today

_____

_____

_____

_____

_____

_____

_____

_____

_____

_____

_____

_____

_____

_____

_____

_____

_____

_____

_____

_____

_____

_____

_____

_____

_____

_____

_____

_____

_____

_____

_____

_____

_____

~August 24

God Will Satisfy You

"I am the LORD your God, who brought you up out of Egypt. Open wide your mouth and I will fill it. But my people would not listen to me; Israel would not submit to me. So I gave them over to their stubborn hearts to follow their own devices. If my people would but listen to me, if Israel would follow my ways, how quickly would I subdue their enemies and turn my hand against their foes! Those who hate the LORD would cringe before him, and their punishment would last forever. But you would be fed with the finest of wheat; with honey from the rock I would satisfy you."

—Psalm 81:10–16

We should never question God's ability and desire to satisfy us when we live in obedience to Him. After all, Jesus said, "Which of you, if his son asks for bread, will give him a stone? Or if he asks for a fish, will give him a snake? If you, then, though you are evil, know how to give good gifts to your children, how much more will your Father in heaven give good gifts to those who ask him!" (Matthew 7:9–11). Those of us who are parents or aunts or uncles know the wonderful feeling we get when we provide for our children and see them trust in us to take care of them. God wants to provide for us in the same way. And not just our food, shelter, and clothing, but the things we *truly* need—love, acceptance, and security. God knows how to satisfy His children. Trust in His promises, obey His commands, and let Him satisfy your hungry heart.

August 25

HOW I CAN DO GOD'S WILL TODAY

_____
_____
_____
_____
_____
_____
_____
_____
_____
_____
_____
_____
_____
_____
_____
_____
_____
_____
_____
_____
_____
_____
_____
_____
_____
_____
_____
_____
_____
_____
_____

August 26

DAVID'S HONORABLE DANCE

David, wearing a linen ephod, danced before the LORD with all his might, while he and the entire house of Israel brought up the ark of the LORD with shouts and the sound of trumpets . . . When David returned home to bless his household, Michal daughter of Saul came out to meet him and said, "How the king of Israel has distinguished himself today, disrobing in the sight of the slave girls of his servants as any vulgar fellow would!" David said to Michal, "It was before the LORD, who chose me rather than your father or anyone from his house when he appointed me ruler over the LORD's people Israel—I will celebrate before the LORD. I will become even more undignified than this, and I will be humiliated in my own eyes. But by these slave girls you spoke of, I will be held in honor."

—2 Samuel 6:14–15, 20–22

David so loved the Father that he danced in the streets even though he was a king. We learn later in this story that because Saul's daughter questioned and ridiculed King David's actions, God struck her so that she could never have children. David's explanation to her about why he was dancing in the street was simple—he was celebrating before the Lord. You see, when you open your heart fully to God, the feeling can be overwhelming! You won't care what other people think about your thoughts or actions or the words that you speak as you praise the Lord. You may be seen as imperfect or even foolish in the eyes of people whose hearts are not devoted to the Father, but God will see your passion shown through your heart and your actions, and you will be praised and rewarded for it by the One who truly gives honor. One other point to learn from this story: don't make fun of how others show their passionate love for God—just imitate it!

August 27

How I Can Do God's Will Today

August 28

SERVING THE WHIMS

It is not fitting for a fool to live in luxury—how much worse for a slave to rule over princes!

—Proverbs 19:10

We claim that we love God's law, but do we? You may live in a home that is completely upside down, where the children rule the parents. The children invite the parents to get with the program or get out of their way. They completely manipulate and use the parents. How does even a one-year-old know that he can accomplish this? Because the child can sense that the parent desires fellowship at almost any cost. The parent adores the child, and the child adores himself—a nice combination for getting what he wants!

How difficult it is to discipline someone whom you adore. Maybe you have struggled with a spoiled child. If the child would only *submit*, there would be peace and blessings for that child. Oh, but no ... temper tantrums, sarcasm, manipulation, demands, and a tossing of the head are all you receive from the spoiled child, instead of the submission, obedience, and loving devotion you so deeply desire. This is a very sick situation to have the creator or parent—the one who brought the child into life—bowing down to the fancy of the child. If it were not for the parent, there would be no child! Yet the parent serves not only the needs, but even the whims of the child.

How awkward to see a parent jumping to a child's commands, or the owner of a business bowing down to the employees, or a husband bowing down to his wife, or a king waiting on his servants as they sit on his throne and demand more from him. All of these pictures make me want to shout out: "Improper! Immoral! Inappropriate! Unseemly!" You must show God that you *do* love His law by putting an end to your rebellion and getting His laws back in order.

August 21

How I Can Do God's Will Today

_____

_____

_____

_____

_____

_____

_____

_____

_____

_____

_____

_____

_____

_____

_____

_____

_____

_____

_____

_____

_____

_____

_____

_____

_____

_____

_____

~August 30

CAUSING A DELAY

Aaron answered them, "Take off the gold earrings that your wives, your sons and your daughters are wearing, and bring them to me." So all the people took off their earrings and brought them to Aaron. He took what they handed him and made it into an idol cast in the shape of a calf, fashioning it with a tool. Then they said, "These are your gods, O Israel, who brought you up out of Egypt."

—Exodus 32:2–4

When I looked, I saw that you had sinned against the LORD your God; you had made for yourselves an idol cast in the shape of a calf. You had turned aside quickly from the way that the LORD had commanded you. So I took the two tablets and threw them out of my hands, breaking them to pieces before your eyes.

—Deuteronomy 9:16–17

Considerable time had passed, and the Israelites did not see Moses coming back down the mountain. Not wanting to bother God in case His watch was broken, they made a golden calf to speed things up. Of course, Israel's worship of the golden calf made God angry. Moses threw down the tablets God had made, breaking them, and the Israelites had to wait another forty days for Moses as he replaced the tablets. We are no different from the Israelites. We, too, are willing to give up our jewelry to keep paying for our false gods and false helpers. We carve out an exercise and diet pill regimen to speed up our journey because we do not *want* to eat less food; we love it too much to eat less of it. I warn you: you will only delay your progress and stay in the desert longer. Truth bears out that false gods *sabotage* us rather than *save* us. Trying to worship God and food at the same time will never work. God is jealous; He knows that false helpers will not help you stop loving your stronghold. You will never truly succeed and be content until you turn to *God* as the Great Physician.

~ August 31

HOW I CAN DO GOD'S WILL TODAY

—September 7

PURSUE HIS RIGHTEOUSNESS AND HIS LOVE

He who pursues righteousness and love finds life, prosperity and honor.
—Proverbs 21:21

Do you ever feel as if nothing is going right, no matter how hard you are trying? You work hard to find success, wealth, and popularity, but no matter how much you achieve, you never feel truly satisfied . . . it's never enough. But if you give your life over to God first, things turn out much differently! If you *pursue* His righteousness and His love, He will give you anything from His storehouse above. No matter what you seek, God gives wonderful gifts if you pursue His will for your life above all else and let *Him* handle all the details!

GIVER OF THINGS
BY GWEN SHAMBLIN

You are the One that I adore/I praise You day by day
You are my love, my heart I pour/Because You light my way

Since You are my love, I hear Your call/You waken me in the night
When I respond I read Your law/And darkness turns to light

If I pursue Your righteousness/And if I pursue Your love
There's nothing that You wouldn't give/From storehouses up above

Chorus: How could I feel this way
            Because You're the King of kings
            How could I feel this great
            Because You are the Giver of things

~ September 2

How I Can Do God's Will Today

— September 3

CONSIDER EACH COMMAND

Love must be sincere. Hate what is evil; cling to what is good. Be devoted to one another in brotherly love. Honor one another above yourselves. Never be lacking in zeal, but keep your spiritual fervor, serving the Lord. Be joyful in hope, patient in affliction, faithful in prayer. Share with God's people who are in need. Practice hospitality.

—Romans 12:9–13

The Bible is absolutely packed with awesome information and direction. There is so much true nutrition for the heart and soul that some paragraphs in the Bible take a whole week to absorb. This one is like that. Spend some time with these words. Consider each command. What are you being asked to do? What does it mean to be devoted, to honor, to keep spiritual fervor? Why is God telling you to share with His people and practice hospitality? God would never ask you to do anything or to direct your heart in a certain direction unless it was truly important to Him. Today, take a few minutes and evaluate your life in regard to this passage. I hope we will all put this into *action*.

~ September 4

How I Can Do God's Will Today

— September 5

HE WANTS TO SAVE US

"You were wearied by all your ways, but you would not say, 'It is hopeless.' You found renewal of your strength, and so you did not faint . . . I will expose your righteousness and your works, and they will not benefit you."

—Isaiah 57:10, 12

God is exposing our righteousness. Right now, many people's righteousness is made up of *making* the rules, then *meeting* the rules. Now they are *self*-righteous—righteous according to the rules they themselves have decided upon. Your ways and your works will not benefit you. You decide on a man-made diet, and yet it does not benefit you. You choose when and what instructions you want to obey from your boss or husband or parent, yet this behavior does not bring peace. You are *self*-right, and this is what Jesus has to say: "Thus you nullify the word of God by your tradition that you have handed down" (Mark 7:13). People who follow diets (not God's laws, but rules handed down by man) nullify God's laws of hunger, fullness, self-control, and having no idols. Do not be greedy—eat only the amount your body needs. You are wearied by all your ways. Turn to God's laws, precepts, and ways, and be saved!

~ September 6

HOW I CAN DO GOD'S WILL TODAY

~September 7

The Gentleman
of All Gentlemen

to him who struck down the firstborn of Egypt	*His love endures forever.*
and brought Israel out from among them	*His love endures forever.*
with a mighty hand and outstretched arm;	*His love endures forever.*
to him who divided the Red Sea asunder	*His love endures forever.*
and brought Israel through the midst of it,	*His love endures forever.*
but swept Pharaoh and his army into the Red Sea;	*His love endures forever.*
to him who led his people through the desert,	*His love endures forever.*
. . . and who gives food to every creature.	*His love endures forever.*

—Psalm 136:10–16, 25

God led His children down to Egypt, and He shook the earth and rescued the Israelites from the clutches of Pharaoh. God parted the Red Sea and took His children across on dry land into the desert with Himself. God never left their presence, for He remained close in the form of a cloud by day and fire by night. He set up examinations for their hearts, put up with the grumbling, prepared disciplining measures for them, and fed them daily with manna from heaven above. God was faithful in battle after battle. And yet He saw that His love and His faithfulness were not enough to pull the heartstrings of mankind to total devotion and love in return. God moved even closer as the Word became flesh and dwelt among men. And even though we showed Him how we really felt by annihilating Him, He remained faithful and desirous of our love. God is the gentleman of all gentlemen, and even in the midst of the grief man has given Him, He extends grace to those who want to put Him back on the throne of their hearts!

~ September 8

HOW I CAN DO GOD'S WILL TODAY

—September 1

THE ONE MIGHTY GOD

The Mighty One, God, the LORD, speaks and summons the earth from the rising of the sun to the place where it sets.

—Psalm 50:1

The voice of the LORD is powerful; the voice of the LORD is majestic. The voice of the LORD breaks the cedars; the LORD breaks in pieces the cedars of Lebanon. He makes Lebanon skip like a calf, Sirion like a young wild ox. The voice of the LORD strikes with flashes of lightning. The voice of the LORD shakes the desert; the LORD shakes the Desert of Kadesh. The voice of the LORD twists the oaks and strips the forests bare. And in his temple all cry, "Glory!"

—Psalm 29:4–9

God controls everything. He has all the power. He is the Creator of the entire earth. So why do you think you will lose time and money if you spend your efforts laying down the worship of a false idol? You will not lose time. Each minute you spend turning your love for a stronghold into love for God will be given back to you—and more. God does not want your money because He is a multibillionaire, and He will reward you with everything you need. You see, God can give all these things back to you because He is the true God and He does not *need* your time or money. When you give of yourself to Him, He will generously give back. No false idol on this earth can do that. Only the one, true, honest-to-goodness *God!* Ascribe to Him the glory due His name (Psalm 29:1–2)!

—September 10

How I Can Do God's Will Today

— September 11

THE GREAT SURGEON

"And you, my son Solomon, acknowledge the God of your father, and serve him with wholehearted devotion and with a willing mind, for the LORD searches every heart and understands every motive behind the thoughts. If you seek him, he will be found by you; but if you forsake him, he will reject you forever."

— *1 Chronicles 28:9*

As you go through the journey in the desert, you may realize several things about your heart that have not occurred to you before. God knows all your thoughts and motives, and He will show you exactly what you have been giving your heart to. His hot desert acts as an X-ray machine, revealing the inner workings of the heart. Don't be afraid for your heart to be revealed. When the Great Surgeon is performing major surgery on your heart, He is making a large incision, removing the pain and the sickness. When He is finished, you have a strong, new heart, able to beat with love for Him! Each of us has the responsibility to get a new heart or attitude toward God as the Boss. As we read earlier in Ezekiel 18:30–32: "Therefore, O house of Israel, I will judge you, each one according to his ways, declares the Sovereign LORD. Repent! Turn away from all your offenses; then sin will not be your downfall. Rid yourselves of all the offenses you have committed, and get a new heart and a new spirit. Why will you die, O house of Israel? For I take no pleasure in the death of anyone, declares the Sovereign LORD. *Repent and live!*"

~ September 12

HOW I CAN DO GOD'S WILL TODAY

September 13

ARE YOU BEARING GOOD FRUIT?

By their fruit you will recognize them. Do people pick grapes from thorn-bushes, or figs from thistles? Likewise every good tree bears good fruit, but a bad tree bears bad fruit. A good tree cannot bear bad fruit, and a bad tree cannot bear good fruit . . . Thus, by their fruit you will recognize them.

—Matthew 7:16–18, 20

You will be sorely attacked when your heart is truly abiding in the Vine. You will be falsely accused, and you will have enemies. You will be able to write your own set of psalms before it is time for you to return home to the Father. Remember, Jesus told us, "If the world hates you, keep in mind that it hated me first. ...If they persecuted me, they will persecute you also" (John 15:18, 20). When the world falsely accuses you and tries to make you out as the troublemaker when you are bringing the sheep back to the Father, the only thing you can hang on to is the *fruit*. These worldly people I am referring to usually attend church every week and can quote scripture just as Satan did to Jesus during His time in the desert. You must look to the Father and check the fruit of your life: love, joy, peace, patience, kindness, goodness, and self-control. Next, look at the fruit of repentance born in others' lives as a result of your loving words from the Father. Please do not get discouraged in doing good, and keep your eyes on the great crowd of witnesses that underwent so much persecution for the sake of Jesus Christ.

P.S. While you're at it, check out the fruit of those who *accuse* the righteous, and you will discover that they have *no* peace, patience, or kindness, but instead are filled with gossip, malice, jealousy, anger, rage, greed, haughtiness, dissension, discord, and involvement in factions. Not very fruitful at all!

—September 14

HOW I CAN DO GOD'S WILL TODAY

~September 15

THE RIGHT KIND OF FEAR

When the people saw the thunder and lightning and heard the trumpet and saw the mountain in smoke, they trembled with fear. They stayed at a distance and said to Moses, "Speak to us yourself and we will listen. But do not have God speak to us or we will die." Moses said to the people, "Do not be afraid. God has come to test you, so that the fear of God will be with you to keep you from sinning."

—Exodus 20:18–20

That was a strange statement: "Do not be *afraid*. God has come to test you, so that the *fear* of God will be with you to keep you from sinning." It was God, trying once more to create an inside force in the heart of man, to place the fear of God in your heart so that you will not want to sin. However, you should not be afraid. In other words, don't have an outside force of fear that terrifies you. That kind of fear doesn't invoke love. But the right kind of fear, an inside force in your heart, can keep you from sinning!

Isaiah wrote a very long vision on a scroll. He said that the key to the treasure of understanding the vision from God is *fear* (Isaiah 33:6). This healthy fear keeps you from foolish ways—running into the street, sleeping on train tracks, defying gravity, and rebelling against God's wishes. Your willingness to obey God reveals the saving fear that is the key to the treasure!

HOW I CAN DO GOD'S WILL TODAY

~September 17

"SEE TO IT"

"No one lights a lamp and puts it in a place where it will be hidden, or under a bowl. Instead he puts it on its stand, so that those who come in may see the light. Your eye is the lamp of your body. When your eyes are good, your whole body also is full of light. But when they are bad, your body also is full of darkness. See to it, then, that the light within you is not darkness. Therefore, if your whole body is full of light, and no part of it dark, it will be completely lighted, as when the light of a lamp shines on you."

—Luke 11:33–36

Someone who loves God more than anything else is a lamp—a light—and should be put on a stand to give direction to everyone in God's house. Each of us has this opportunity to shine as a lamp for God. This opportunity is already within us. But then Jesus warned us to *see to it* that the light within us is not darkness. It is not just an opportunity to shine for the Lord; it is a direction from Jesus. He warned us that we should never become overly confident that our hearts are pure and our lights shine bright. Instead, we should stay on our knees and in His Word to be diligent that there is no darkness in our hearts.

—September 18

How I Can Do God's Will Today

_____
_____
_____
_____
_____
_____
_____
_____
_____
_____
_____
_____
_____
_____
_____
_____
_____
_____
_____
_____
_____
_____
_____
_____
_____
_____
_____
_____
_____
_____
_____

~September 11

THE OPPORTUNITY
IN THE DESERT

How often they rebelled against him in the desert and grieved him in the wasteland! Again and again they put God to the test; they vexed the Holy One of Israel. They did not remember his power—the day he redeemed them from the oppressor, the day he displayed his miraculous signs in Egypt.

—Psalm 78:40–43a

When you leave Egypt, you really discover how much of your heart is buried in the pyramids, which are presently in the shape of a pantry and a refrigerator. God has brought you to the desert—a place designed just for you and Him, with no room for worldly idols. But you learn something very disturbing about your heart in the desert, far away from the familiar food scene . . . your heart is not satisfied with *only* God. God alone isn't enough, and you want more. You want your food, too. It is a tough lesson to learn, but if you remain focused on God, you will turn it around. This desert of testing and self-denial is an opportunity—not a curse—an *opportunity* to learn much about the Father and yourself. As you learn these things about yourself and you give your heart, soul, mind, and strength to the Father, He will give you *everything* back. His rewards will be great, and you will sing of His glory!

—September 20

HOW I CAN DO GOD'S WILL TODAY

~ September 21

PUT YOUR CHILDREN IN HIS HANDS

*In bitterness of soul Hannah wept much and prayed to the LORD. And
she made a vow, saying, "O LORD Almighty, if you will only look upon
your servant's misery and remember me, and not forget your servant
but give her a son, then I will give him to the LORD for all the days of
his life, and no razor will ever be used on his head."*

—1 Samuel 1:10–11

*He [David] answered, "While the child was still alive, I fasted and
wept. I thought, 'Who knows? The LORD may be gracious to me and let
the child live.' But now that he is dead, why should I fast? Can I bring
him back again? I will go to him, but he will not return to me."*

—2 Samuel 12:22–23

If you are a parent, God has placed you in a position of authority and caregiving over your children. But you must remember that they are, first and foremost, *His* children, and He will provide for them in all ways. Like Hannah, you must be willing to say to God that your children belong to Him for all the days of their lives. Be in constant prayer for guidance about how to raise, discipline, and teach your children, for God alone has the perfect plan.

You must also be at peace about God's will for your children. Like David, pray for the strength, health, and safety of your children, but if God's plan is different, accept His will with faith and trust, and He will comfort your soul. If you follow God's plan for you as a parent by seeking His guidance in loving, teaching, and disciplining your children, you will be on the right path. Even during times when you feel that the world is passing you and your children by, if you have chosen a trusting, humble path, you will look up and see that your children's gifts are many, their relationship with God is strong, and their days are filled with peace and joy!

— September 22

HOW I CAN DO GOD'S WILL TODAY

~ September 23

LIKE MOTHER, LIKE DAUGHTER
LIKE FATHER, LIKE SON

I have been reminded of your sincere faith, which first lived in your grandmother Lois and in your mother Eunice and, I am persuaded, now lives in you also.

—2 Timothy 1:5

"Everyone who quotes proverbs will quote this proverb about you: 'Like mother, like daughter.'"

—Ezekiel 16:44

Besides the misplaced devotion to food, parents often secretly hold within their hearts the pursuit of money and the praise of men. Children will pick up on the diametric goals of the parents who go to church, yet pursue money or aspire to climb the social ladder. If only parents could see that they are forcing the ungodly and unrewarding preoccupation with money and praise on their children. God will frustrate their goals. These confused parents want to live vicariously through their children because they are greedy for attention and praise from mankind. When parents mistakenly create goals for their children that are not forsaking-all-and-knowing-Christ goals, by the time the children reach their teens, they are very confused, unhappy, and emotional, often having fits of anger and tears. Depression surfaces from time to time when they stop to realize that they are empty and getting nowhere. These children soon mimic their parents' pursuits, spending their energy and strength to strive toward worldly goals every day. They expect that they can "make" things happen for them with their raw talent. Pride sets in. A powerful little god of SELF is birthed and, as the old saying goes, "like mother, like daughter—like father, like son." We must check our hearts and motives!

— September 24

How I Can Do God's Will Today

~September 25

FINDING THE RIGHT PATH

I am your servant; give me discernment that I may understand your statutes. It is time for you to act, O LORD; your law is being broken. Because I love your commands more than gold, more than pure gold, and because I consider all your precepts right, I hate every wrong path.
—Psalm 119:125–128

The Bible helps us find the right path that will lead us straight to the heart of the Father. It helps us circumvent the mountains and valleys, and it provides street lamps for dark paths. It helps us avoid the dreadful parts of the desert that are thirsty and waterless. It helps us evade the scorpions, snakes, sandpits, and desert storms. If we do not stay in His Word and honor His precepts—shouting them from the street corner, writing them on the doorposts, and talking about them when we are going in and coming out—then, my friend, we will forfeit peace, and it will cost us dearly at times. If we are not careful, we might walk some of the wicked desert paths that the Israelites walked. Therefore, we must learn from history and remember that God's grace and mercy are new every morning, and like the psalmist, we must *hate* every wrong path and *never* want to walk there!

—September 26

How I Can Do God's Will Today

~September 27

DON'T LOOK BACK

"Woe to the obstinate children," declares the LORD, "to those who carry out plans that are not mine, forming an alliance, but not by my Spirit, heaping sin upon sin; who go down to Egypt without consulting me; who look for help to Pharaoh's protection, to Egypt's shade for refuge. But Pharaoh's protection will be to your shame, Egypt's shade will bring you disgrace."

—Isaiah 30:1–3

God has delivered you from having to serve your strongholds and false idols, and now you have the chance to serve Him. That is the grace of God through Jesus Christ. Times may get tough, and facing those tests is part of the hot desert. But don't even entertain the thought of returning to Egypt, depending upon the aid of man or pills or other things to "save you" from your situation. Where does your mind go when you see the scales go up or you backslide on your stronghold? *That* is your Egypt.

If you are tempted, take time to remember all the trials and bondage of being enslaved to your stronghold, such as monthly fad diets, denied foods, dangerous pills, mandatory exercise routines, and clothes that don't fit. Nothing is there for you in Egypt, and you will regret the wasted time you spend relying upon a false help. Spare yourself the trouble—trust in God, and never look back to Egypt! *God* is your Savior! Read what He says in Isaiah: "'I, even I, am the LORD, and apart from me there is no savior. I have revealed and saved and proclaimed—I, and not some foreign god among you. You are my witnesses,' declares the LORD, 'that I am God. Yes, and from ancient days I am he. No one can deliver out of my hand. When I act, *who can reverse it?*'" (Isaiah 43:11–13)

—September 28

How I Can Do God's Will Today

— September 21

EVERYTHING WE NEED FOR GODLINESS

His divine power has given us everything we need for life and godliness through our knowledge of him who called us by his own glory and goodness. Through these he has given us his very great and precious promises, so that through them you may participate in the divine nature and escape the corruption in the world caused by evil desires.

—2 Peter 1:3–4

Quit looking for one more person or book or formula that is going to make you lose weight or that will help you with your stronghold. Don't you see? Through God, we *have everything we need for life and godliness. Everything!* He has given us a means by which we can escape the corruption caused by our evil desires. So why do we continue to seek other methods? Methods such as constant dieting do not help us escape our evil desires; they only lead us farther into them by making us fall more in love with food! God has already given you what you need for godliness. And that means *godliness!* You can escape the corruption of this world caused by your evil desires and participate in God's divine nature. Now read 2 Peter 1:5–11: "For this very reason, make every effort to add to your faith goodness; and to goodness, knowledge; and to knowledge, self-control; and to self-control, perseverance; and to perseverance, godliness; and to godliness, brotherly kindness; and to brotherly kindness, love. For if you possess these qualities in increasing measure, they will keep you from being ineffective and unproductive in your knowledge of our Lord Jesus Christ. But if anyone does not have them, he is nearsighted and blind, and has forgotten that he has been cleansed from his past sins. Therefore, my brothers, be all the more eager to make your calling and election sure. For if you do these things, you will never fall, and you will receive a rich welcome into the eternal kingdom of our Lord and Savior Jesus Christ."

~ *September 30*

How I Can Do God's Will Today

_____

_____

_____

_____

_____

_____

_____

_____

_____

_____

_____

_____

_____

_____

_____

_____

_____

_____

_____

_____

_____

_____

_____

_____

_____

_____

—October 7

THE FOUR SOILS
(THE FOUR HEARTS)

Then he told them many things in parables, saying: "A farmer went out to sow his seed. As he was scattering the seed, some fell along the path, and the birds came and ate it up. Some fell on rocky places, where it did not have much soil. It sprang up quickly, because the soil was shallow. But when the sun came up, the plants were scorched, and they withered because they had no root. Other seed fell among thorns, which grew up and choked the plants. Still other seed fell on good soil, where it produced a crop—a hundred, sixty or thirty times what was sown. He who has ears, let him hear."

—Matthew 13:3–9

I think I have figured out one of the reasons that some people feel at arm's length from God. Read what Jesus said about the four soils. This passage can actually describe the different types of hearts on this earth. You see, the seed is God's kingdom of love, the soil is a heart of love, and the rock is a heart of hate, the antithesis of love. Love cannot root in hate. In the first heart, the seeds were scattered—not listened to or given a chance. The second heart had *some* ability to respond to the love, and the love sprouted toward God, but because hate, jealousy, and anger were solidly fixed in the rocky heart, the love could not take root. The third soil was a heart of love ... but it also loved the world ... but it loved God ... but it loved the world ... but it loved God. At first, it grew in love toward the Father and became a plant; but where the heart is divided, the world will always win, and the world squeezed out the love for the Father. You cannot have two masters (Matthew 6:24). We must believe in God. Repent from these behaviors that are the antithesis of a belief in God, and watch your heart grow in love. Watch His kingdom grow in your heart, like the good heart that produced fruit a hundredfold!

—October 2

HOW I CAN DO GOD'S WILL TODAY

—October 3

LOOK FOR THE OASIS

"'You yourselves have seen what I did to Egypt, and how I carried you on eagles' wings and brought you to myself.'"

—Exodus 19:4

God rescued the Israelites from Egypt and then started testing them right off the bat. For the first three days of wandering in the desert, they found no water. When they finally found water, it was too bitter to drink. They failed the trust test, but God miraculously made the water sweet and then led them to not one, but *twelve* springs of water and seventy palm trees (Exodus 15:22–27).

This desert exam—even though it was resolved and followed by an oasis—never sank into the hearts of the Israelites. They never connected that God was going to take them to the edge of death and then rescue them at the twelfth hour. Are you learning that God will take you to the edge of death with your stronghold and then rescue you in an amazing way? You will experience desert oasis after desert oasis. Learn to trust Him and show it by your continued submission and obedience, until you get to a point that you will joyfully say, "Where, O death, is your victory? Where, O death, is your sting?" (1 Corinthians 15:55).

—October 4

How I Can Do God's Will Today

~ October 5

PRESS ON TOWARD THE GOAL

My dear children, I write this to you so that you will not sin. But if any-body does sin, we have one who speaks to the Father in our defense—Jesus Christ, the Righteous One. He is the atoning sacrifice for our sins, and not only for ours but also for the sins of the whole world.

— 1 John 2:1–2

When you mess up and find that the gravity of sin has pulled your face back down into your plate or into the refrigerator or has made you drive your car to the fast-food restaurant even though you are not hungry, you need to refocus. Get down on your knees and pray. Forget what is behind you, look toward what is ahead, and ask God to refocus your mind. Do not wait until Monday morning to refocus—do it now. People who wait are announcing the deep feelings in their hearts; they do not want to let go of food. Why would you wait till tomorrow if you really felt sad and wanted to get it right for God? Take your focus off your greedy desires because they are the opposite of God's. Keep your Bible with you at all times, so the truth about what God wants for your life is always nearby.

—October 6

HOW I CAN DO GOD'S WILL TODAY

~October 7

A TREASURED PASSION

Now if you obey me fully and keep my covenant, then out of all nations you will be my treasured possession. Although the whole earth is mine, you will be for me a kingdom of priests and a holy nation.

—Exodus 19:5–6a

As time goes by, some of us might find ourselves plateaued in the desert. The next thing we know, we haven't lost weight for weeks, which may turn into months, which may turn into years. We have thought that since we have plateaued and are feeling pain again after the honeymoon, it must be the heat of the desert. We say, "Oh, it's just one of those desert storms. God is just working on me. I'm waiting on the Lord. He is working on something else in my life right now. He will complete the work He started."

Yes, you will struggle in the desert, but true desert struggles are the pain and suffering from *obedience,* not the pain that comes from hugging the refrigerator and trying to get God to repent or change His mind so that you can have two masters. Desert pain is not the pain of disobedience! Remember, those who were disobedient *died in the desert.* But if you fully obey His commands, you will be a treasured possession who knows you have the right to choose full obedience. Anyone in awe of God and His precepts will obey Him. Remember what Jesus said in John 14:15, 21: "If you love me, you will obey what I command. ...Whoever has my commands and obeys them, he is the one who loves me."

—October 8

HOW I CAN DO GOD'S WILL TODAY

—October 9

VINE AND BRANCHES

"I am the vine; you are the branches. If a man remains in me and I in him, he will bear much fruit; apart from me you can do nothing. If anyone does not remain in me, he is like a branch that is thrown away and withers; such branches are picked up, thrown into the fire and burned. If you remain in me and my words remain in you, ask whatever you wish, and it will be given you."

—John 15:5–7

It is one thing to *come* to Christ, but it is another thing to *remain* in Christ. Both the King James Version and the New King James Version of the Bible use the phrase "abide in me." Christ said "if" you abide in Him. If you do not remain in Him (and obviously you have the choice not to), then the picture is not pretty. You need to stay totally focused on the mind and heart of Jesus Christ. *Abide* or *remain* means "to stick around"—"to stay put"—with Jesus as Lord, not vice versa. The branches get life from the vine; they get all the material they need for life from one source. Likewise, we cannot look for life in multiple places. You will know when you have figured out what *abide* means because you will constantly receive answers to your prayers. "If you remain in me and my words remain in you, ask whatever you wish, and it will be given you."

~October 10

How I Can Do God's Will Today

HAS YOUR CONSCIENCE BEEN SEARED?

Such teachings come through hypocritical liars, whose consciences have been seared as with a hot iron.

— 1 Timothy 4:2

I tell you this, and insist on it in the Lord, that you must no longer live as the Gentiles do, in the futility of their thinking. They are darkened in their understanding and separated from the life of God because of the ignorance that is in them due to the hardening of their hearts. Having lost all sensitivity, they have given themselves over to sensuality so as to indulge in every kind of impurity, with a continual lust for more. You, however, did not come to know Christ that way. Surely you heard of him and were taught in him in accordance with the truth that is in Jesus. You were taught, with regard to your former way of life, to put off your old self, which is being corrupted by its deceitful desires; to be made new in the attitude of your minds; and to put on the new self, created to be like God in true righteousness and holiness. Therefore each of you must put off falsehood and speak truthfully to his neighbor, for we are all members of one body. "In your anger do not sin": Do not let the sun go down while you are still angry, and do not give the devil a foothold.

—Ephesians 4:17–27

Many will guiltily beg God to please love them but let them keep their other loves too! But if we continue in sinful behavior, we will eventually become callous and have no more guilty feelings because our consciences will have been seared. What a frightening thought! You do not want it both ways—you will be miserable. Jesus redeemed us and set us *apart* to love the Father. In Titus 2 we learn that Jesus gave Himself to redeem us from all wickedness and to purify God's people; because of this, we should be *eager* to do what is pleasing to God. Each of us must put on a new self—this self that has been given through God's grace. We were *made* to do this.

—October 12

How I Can Do God's Will Today

—October 13

DESERT DISCIPLINE

Remember how the LORD your God led you all the way in the desert these forty years, to humble you and to test you in order to know what was in your heart, whether or not you would keep his commands. He humbled you, causing you to hunger and then feeding you with manna, which neither you nor your fathers had known, to teach you that man does not live on bread alone but on every word that comes from the mouth of the LORD. Your clothes did not wear out and your feet did not swell during these forty years. Know then in your heart that as a man disciplines his son, so the LORD your God disciplines you.

—Deuteronomy 8:2–5

The desert is a place of discipline. That doesn't mean you are a failure. Satan loves for you to think that you are, and he loves for you to ignore the truth that you are a prize to be won. You are popular! But God disciplines His children out of love and concern. However, Satan knows that you can get distracted easily and mistake the discipline of God for a lack of love. How "opposite world" can you get! Stick to the truth, and don't listen to anything the king of lies has to say. Anyone investing attention toward you loves you, and who has invested more attention in you during your lifetime than the great God Almighty?

—October 14

HOW I CAN DO GOD'S WILL TODAY

~October 15

WHOLEHEARTED DEVOTION

Be diligent in these matters; give yourself wholly to them, so that every-one may see your progress. Watch your life and doctrine closely. Persevere in them, because if you do, you will save both yourself and your hearers.

— 1 Timothy 4:15–16

I am saying this for your own good, not to restrict you, but that you may live in a right way in undivided devotion to the Lord.

— 1 Corinthians 7:35

If you believe in something, you want to surround yourself totally with its teaching—absorbing, imitating, and baptizing yourself into the philosophy. For many of us, we have believed in the man-made diet rules and regulations. We have studied every new diet, analyzed every bite of food, and committed to memory various exercise routines. But now you have something new to believe in. Instead of throwing yourself into any more diet books, food measurements, and fat grams, throw yourself into absorbing the life, the heart, the obedience, the humility, the submissiveness, and the love of Jesus. The rewards for imitating and following Jesus will be more fulfilling than you can imagine! No matter what your stronghold, start today by transferring the old devotion to total devotion to God by imitating whom God adored: Jesus Christ. Imitate His devotion to the Word of God. By twelve years old, He could debate the Word. Imitate His submission to parents and to God—even when it went against His will. Jesus' humble response: *not My will but Yours, Father.* That is wholehearted devotion when you lay down your life for God's truth and His will.

~October 16

How I Can Do God's Will Today

~ October 17

"LEAVE ROOM FOR GOD'S WRATH"

Do not repay anyone evil for evil. Be careful to do what is right in the eyes of everybody. If it is possible, as far as it depends on you, live at peace with everyone. Do not take revenge, my friends, but leave room for God's wrath, for it is written: "It is mine to avenge; I will repay," says the Lord. On the contrary: "If your enemy is hungry, feed him; if he is thirsty, give him something to drink. In doing this, you will heap burning coals on his head." Do not be overcome by evil, but overcome evil with good.

—Romans 12:17–21

Give up your need to win verbally. Stay peaceful and confident that God will take care of others who are doing wrong to you. God will be quick to correct and take revenge if you give Him room, but He does not gang up on people. If you talk back or take revenge, then He won't get involved. Another hint is this: He will not let your clever words or defense be effective. *He* wants to take care of us, so put away your pocketknife and let Him use His powerful sword and His enormous army!

It is clear in the scriptures that the biggest attack to those who are trying to walk a "blameless life" includes slander and false accusations. David wrote the majority of the Psalms to praise God. However, much of the praise and prayer was for God to set the enemies down that slandered him. Read Psalms 58, 59, 60, 119, and 140. Notice that the enemy slandered, but in each case, David ran to God and His Word.

The arrogant mock me without restraint, but I do not turn from your law.

—Psalm 119:51

~October 18

How I Can Do God's Will Today

~October 11

MAKE MUSIC IN YOUR HEART

Sing for joy to God our strength; shout aloud to the God of Jacob! Begin the music, strike the tambourine, play the melodious harp and lyre.

—Psalm 81:1–2

Speak to one another with psalms, hymns and spiritual songs. Sing and make music in your heart to the Lord....

—Ephesians 5:19

K ing Saul summoned David to come and play the harp and sing to drive the evil spirits away. Satan is very jealous, and he cannot stand to hear the saints sing to the Father. There are many references in the Bible commanding us to sing to God and shout to God and to begin the music and strike the tambourine. I have never needed prompting for this command because God has the perfect blend of leadership, genius, and power as well as kindness and thoughtfulness. How can I help but to sing praises to Him in joy? We all need to do more of it, even if we don't think we can sing, especially while we are in the hot desert!

Declare to the heavenly realm and the evil forces of the spiritual realm that we are *blessed* to have life at all and that the light and momentary troubles *do not compare* to the riches of our inheritance! If you will be still long enough to really imagine eternal life with this wonderful God, you will have reason to sing!

—October 20

HOW I CAN DO GOD'S WILL TODAY

—October 21

"Is the Lord Among Us or Not?"

The LORD answered Moses, "Walk on ahead of the people. Take with you some of the elders of Israel and take in your hand the staff with which you struck the Nile, and go. I will stand there before you by the rock at Horeb. Strike the rock, and water will come out of it for the people to drink." So Moses did this in the sight of the elders of Israel. And he called the place Massah and Meribah because the Israelites quarreled and because they tested the LORD saying, "Is the LORD among us or not?"

—Exodus 17:5-7

Let's dissect this new attitude. Their big question was, "Is the LORD among us or not?" I don't think for one minute that the children of God doubted the existence of God. That was not the problem. Look at the Israelites' question again: "Is the LORD among us or not?" What were they talking about? Could it be that those arrogant children of God were saying, "Is God *with* us or not?" Or better yet, "Is He going to get with the program or not? He is either with us or against us. Is God going to submit to our wants or not?" They had no use for a God who was not going to serve their cravings. They were not so sure that Jehovah was working out! Is God among us or not?

The state of the heart of man is more unmanageable and unruly than first thought; there are hearts that actually want God to *repent* if He is going to hang around! After all, they always have Egypt to run to if God doesn't give them what they want! We should make sure that we don't ever ask God to repent or make Him angry by asking Him to do things our way. *He is the Boss; we are not.*

—October 22

HOW I CAN DO GOD'S WILL TODAY

_____
_____
_____
_____
_____
_____
_____
_____
_____
_____
_____
_____
_____
_____
_____
_____
_____
_____
_____
_____
_____
_____
_____
_____
_____
_____
_____
_____
_____
_____
_____
_____

~October 23

SATAN'S LIES AND THE FALSE PROPHETS

This is what the LORD Almighty says: "Do not listen to what the prophets are prophesying to you; they fill you with false hopes. They speak visions from their own minds, not from the mouth of the LORD. They keep saying to those who despise me, 'The LORD says: You will have peace.' And to all who follow the stubbornness of their hearts they say, 'No harm will come to you.' But which of them has stood in the council of the LORD to see or to hear his word?"

—Jeremiah 23:16–18a

We need to make it a priority to know where our hearts are, just as we want to know where our children are at night. We also need to recognize that Satan is a big, fat liar who will always tell us that we are somewhere we are not. To make a dent in this overwhelming delusion brought upon God's people, let's learn about Satan's lies and be aware of false prophets. In other words, Satan is telling us that we are saved from loving the world. Satan tells us, "You are doing fine . . . you don't love the world." False prophets back him up and tell you that you are in God's favor and abiding in Christ, even as your heart continues to sin. If the human heart is so easily deceived, then we of *all* people should be the *most* mindful, careful, watchful, leery, observant, open-eyed, conscientious, and cautious group of people—able to identify exactly the treasures of our hearts, because, as it says in Matthew 6:21, "For where your treasure is, there your heart will be also." Read all of Jeremiah 23 and note verse 14. It says that false preachers of the day actually *strengthen* the hand of the sinner instead of turning him from sin. Stay awake!

—October 24

HOW I CAN DO GOD'S WILL TODAY

~ October 25

The Grass Is Greener in Your Own Yard

"'You adulterous wife! You prefer strangers to your own husband! Every prostitute receives a fee, but you give gifts to all your lovers, bribing them to come to you from everywhere for your illicit favors. So in your prostitution you are the opposite of others; no one runs after you for your favors. You are the very opposite, for you give payment and none is given to you.'"

—Ezekiel 16:32–34

God called Himself many things to help us understand His intimate love and concern for us. One of the things is "husband-defender." In the book of Hosea, you see the allegory of how we are hurting God by running to other lovers. This passage from Ezekiel points out, "You [the Israelites] prefer strangers to your own husband [referring to Himself]!" What happens in a marriage when one partner looks beyond the vow of love, wanting attention from strangers more than from the spouse? The "grass is greener on the other side of the fence" syndrome is false. Once you cross the fence and get close to the grass, it loses that dark green color, and you see what it really is—brown and full of weeds. And when you look back to your own yard, your grass looks greener than it ever did before. Don't believe the lie of Satan. You should have faith that God has given you wonderful, green, healthy grass in your own yard. The spouse God has given you is better than any other spouse out there, and your God is better than any other god. He is the great I AM. Open your eyes, see what a treasure He is, and appreciate what you have, or else He might take things away from you. Be content with what you have.

—October 26

How I Can Do God's Will Today

_____

_____

_____

_____

_____

_____

_____

_____

_____

_____

_____

_____

_____

_____

_____

_____

_____

_____

_____

_____

_____

_____

_____

_____

_____

_____

_____

~ October 27

SHOULD YOU BE AFRAID?

For rulers hold no terror for those who do right, but for those who do wrong. Do you want to be free from fear of the one in authority? Then do what is right and he will commend you. For he is God's servant to do you good. But if you do wrong, be afraid, for he does not bear the sword for nothing. He is God's servant, an agent of wrath to bring punishment on the wrongdoer. Therefore, it is necessary to submit to the authorities, not only because of possible punishment but also because of conscience.

—Romans 13:3–5

Do you know someone at your workplace who always seems to be worried about getting in trouble, even when he feels that he is doing everything he should? Are *you* one of the people who feels this way? This passage from Romans should be very important to you. Think about it. When you do what is right, you don't have to worry about your boss or leader. However, if you do what is wrong, the Bible says to "be afraid." If you are praying for God's guidance and doing the best you can do, you have no need to be afraid around your boss or supervisor. But search your heart. If you are doing what is wrong or if you are trying to get away with as much as you can, then you *do* have reason to be afraid. In that case, the Bible says to "be afraid."

Please remember the following: "Everyone must submit himself to the governing authorities, for there is no authority except that which God has established. The authorities that exist have been established by God. Consequently, he who rebels against the authority is rebelling against what God has instituted, and those who do so will bring judgment on themselves" (Romans 13:1–2).

—October 28

How I Can Do God's Will Today

— October 21

YOU ARE PRICELESS

"Are not two sparrows sold for a penny? Yet not one of them will fall to the ground apart from the will of your Father. And even the very hairs of your head are all numbered. So don't be afraid; you are worth more than many sparrows."

—Matthew 10:29–31

God feeds and cares for the birds of the air, and He dresses the lilies of the field in splendor. How much more do you think He cares for us, people whom He created in His own image? Jesus Himself told us that we are worth more than many sparrows. Actually I think it is almost impossible for our limited hearts and minds to comprehend the kind of attention that God gives us each day. He knows how many hairs you have on your head today. He knows things about you that *you* don't know. How have we taken this for granted? How have we missed it? We are all blessed to be alive, much less to be adored as we are!

If you think that God has forsaken you, then seek Him with all of your heart. The truth is that *you* have forsaken *Him*. God *opposes* the proud (James 4:6). But remember, the proud don't need a god and don't have to obey the one true God. They can do what they want and eat what they want and lust when they want. Once again they have forsaken the concept of *God first*. Humble yourself, for God gives salvation to the humble.

—October 30

How I Can Do God's Will Today

— October 31

Is Your Heart Lukewarm?

"I know your deeds, that you are neither cold nor hot. I wish you were either one or the other! So, because you are lukewarm—neither hot nor cold—I am about to spit you out of my mouth. You say, 'I am rich; I have acquired wealth and do not need a thing.' But you do not realize that you are wretched, pitiful, poor, blind and naked."

—Revelation 3:15–17

"Those whom I love I rebuke and discipline. So be earnest, and repent. Here I am! I stand at the door and knock. If anyone hears my voice and opens the door, I will come in and eat with him, and he with me."

—Revelation 3:19–20

The torture zone is a condition of the heart that is neither hot nor cold—it is lukewarm. That was the condition of the church of Laodicea to whom this message was written in Revelation. The most torturous place is in the middle of the road, where you don't have strong feelings in any direction. You feel a little guilty and feel like you probably *should* get rid of sin in your life, but that it really is okay to keep living like that, because God will understand, and after all, everybody else does it. But God reveals His feelings about someone with this type of heart: He states that *He will spit you out of His mouth!* When you are floundering between one state or the other, God is upset with you, and you don't even like yourself. If you find yourself in this condition, pray that God will reveal the direction you should go and the attitude you should have. He is knocking at the door of your heart even as you are reading this. Let Him in. If He is in your heart, He will be in the foremost position there, for He is God. Open up, submit, and then you will enjoy this relationship, and it will be strong!

November 7

HOW I CAN DO GOD'S WILL TODAY

November 2

THE KINGDOM BELONGS
TO SUCH AS THESE

People were bringing little children to Jesus to have him touch them, but the disciples rebuked them. When Jesus saw this, he was indignant. He said to them, "Let the little children come to me, and do not hinder them, for the kingdom of God belongs to such as these."

—Mark 10:13–14

We have seen examples of small children, even as young as two years old, who realize that we are supposed to eat only when our stomachs are hungry because that is the way God made us. You know, it is amazing that such truth comes naturally from the mouths of babes. The concept of waiting on God for everything, including food, is such a simple idea and is characteristic of a child's heart. We need to relearn this basic Christian concept, and we can learn it easily by watching our young children. At the same time, we should encourage our children to keep that trusting attitude of "let go and let God." As many of us have realized lately, it is much easier to *keep* the right attitude than it is to relearn it later in life!

November 3

How I Can Do God's Will Today

November 4

ONLY A DAY?

"'Why have we fasted,' they say, 'and you have not seen it? Why have we humbled ourselves, and you have not noticed?' Yet on the day of your fasting, you do as you please . . . You cannot fast as you do today and expect your voice to be heard on high. Is this the kind of fast I have chosen, only a day for a man to humble himself?"

—Isaiah 58:3a, 4b–5a

Put yourself in God's place. He made you, and your body is His temple. He should rightfully make decisions daily of how His creation should respond to Him. Now is it for a *day* that God wants you to move off the throne of your heart and let Him rule? Does He get to rule only *a day*? And does He want you to cry on the days that He makes the decision about how much food you are to eat? Do you humble yourself in the morning hours and then push God off the throne in the evening hours with decisions of how much food you are going to binge on and how much you are going to run your mouth? We all know better. We *must* allow God to be God and let Him rule twenty-four hours a day, seven days a week.

HOW I CAN DO GOD'S WILL TODAY

November 6

EVERYONE MUST SUBMIT

Everyone must submit himself to the governing authorities, for there is no authority except that which God has established. The authorities that exist have been established by God. Consequently, he who rebels against the authority is rebelling against what God has instituted....

—Romans 13:1–2a

*G*overning authority means any person who has authority over you. For a child, that might mean his parents or occasionally an older brother. For a wife, her husband. For a working man, his boss, whether the boss is male or female. Our authorities must submit to their authorities. Everyone should submit because God is speaking through the voice of the ruling authority. Submitting is easy when things are going well and when the authority over you has the same priorities and desires that you do. But many times, submission is tough because the desires of the authority go against our desires. We must remember that the Father planned this, too. Even when the Israelites were taken into captivity by abusive rulers, God allowed that to happen so that the Israelites would ultimately and eventually have the right attitude of submission toward Him. If things seem tough or trying, we must submit to our governing authorities, or we directly rebel against the plan that God has arranged. God will take care of you. Try it.

Consider Colossians 3:22: "Slaves, obey your earthly masters in everything; and do it, not only when their eye is on you and to win their favor, but with sincerity of heart and reverence for the Lord." It is the Lord you are serving through your earthly authority. Colossians 3:25 states that if either the employer or employee does wrong, he will be repaid—so why fret or resist?

November 7

HOW I CAN DO GOD'S WILL TODAY

November 8

I'D LOVE TO SEE
GOD ON THE NEWS

LORD, I have heard of your fame; I stand in awe of your deeds, O LORD. Renew them in our day, in our time make them known; in wrath remember mercy.

—*Habakkuk 3:2*

It really bothers me that God is not in the headline news every night. I would love to hear a newscaster say, "And the hand of God spared this person from a fatal accident."

It makes me mad that God is not on the weather channel every night. Can you imagine hearing the weatherman say, "And God did something new again. We guessed that it was going to rain today, but God decided to bring sunshine instead. What a God of surprises He is! Did anyone see the sunset He painted yesterday? He outdid Himself again."

Why is God not given credit in all the science books and research? Instead, everyone loves to chalk it all up to "Mother Nature." Oh, don't even get me started! My whole soul flares up within me when I get on this subject. Let us all pray, as the prophet Habakkuk did centuries ago, for this arrogant generation. Strive to begin each day standing in awe of God's deeds, and give *Him* credit where all credit and honor and praise are due!

November 9

How I Can Do God's Will Today

November 10

You Cannot Camouflage Your Heart

The only thing that counts is faith expressing itself through love.

—Galatians 5:6b

It is true that you cannot do works and get away with disguising the absence of love in your heart. Attempting to camouflage your heart will not get you into God's presence. Do you want a marriage partner who does things around you and for you, but who does not genuinely care for you? Of course not! God is no different. Well, what about halfway loving God? Is that okay? Should you continue loving your worldly lovers while God is madly in love with you? In other words, should you continue in sin that grace may abound? Romans 6:2 has the answer: "By no means!"

God has gotten down on His knees (so to speak) to propose to you when you consider that He sacrificed His only Son for your hand in marriage or this covenant relationship. How can you turn this down or run after another lover? This proposal from God demands a response of wholehearted love and faith from us. Throughout the Old and New Testaments, God gets upset at His children for turning to another lover (idol), much less trying to talk Him into letting all three get into the same bed. That has always been our problem—we want God to let us have our lovers and still be pleased with us. Give it up . . . He never will.

November 11

HOW I CAN DO GOD'S WILL TODAY

November 12

YOU ARE NOT FAR

"Well said, teacher," the man replied. "You are right in saying that God is one and there is no other but him. To love him with all your heart, with all your understanding and with all your strength, and to love your neighbor as yourself is more important than all burnt offerings and sacrifices." When Jesus saw that he had answered wisely, he said to him, "You are not far from the kingdom of God." And from then on no one dared ask him any more questions.

—Mark 12:32–34

Why did Jesus say, "You are not far from the kingdom of God"? Couldn't He have told the man who answered wisely, "You hit the nail on the head; you understand it and you have got it"? Having the *knowledge* of what God is looking for is a beginning, but it is not enough. The journey has to start with the mind, as we discussed before, but it must lead to the *heart*. You can have the knowledge of God, yet not have a heart for Him. Begin your journey today learning about God's lessons, and start loving God with all your heart! Isn't it wonderful that Jesus summed up the law and all the words of the prophets by saying to love God with your heart, soul, and mind, and love your neighbor as yourself? If we would really take this passage to heart, we would not be far from the kingdom of God.

How I Can Do God's Will Today

_____

_____

_____

_____

_____

_____

_____

_____

_____

_____

_____

_____

_____

_____

_____

_____

_____

_____

_____

_____

_____

_____

_____

_____

_____

_____

_____

_____

_____

_____

_____

November 14

LET NO DEBT REMAIN

Give everyone what you owe him: If you owe taxes, pay taxes; if rev-
enue, then revenue; if respect, then respect; if honor, then honor. Let
no debt remain outstanding, except the continuing debt to love one
another, for he who loves his fellowman has fulfilled the law.

—Romans 13:7–8

Jesus told us in the New Testament that we should love our neigh-
bors as ourselves. This statement encompasses a lot of things, but
one thing it certainly means is that you should give others what is
due them: money, time, attention, respect, acclaim, appreciation, or
anything. How have you been treating the people in your family, at
church, in your neighborhood, and at work? To whom have you
shown heartfelt love and concern today? Pay no mind to the way
that others treat you, for Jesus was a great example of the way to love
others even when we are not shown love by them. Instead, commit
your heart to showing love to your fellowman, for by this you will be
fulfilling God's law. Much of the religious teachings of the day tell
people to work on self-esteem, but this focus is not found in the
Word of God. The reason is that we feed ourselves, dress ourselves,
bathe ourselves—we automatically love ourselves. Our job is to obey
our Boss, and *He* will build our self-esteem and fulfill our need for
acceptance. Let no debt remain except the continuing debt to love.

November 15

HOW I CAN DO GOD'S WILL TODAY

_____

_____

_____

_____

_____

_____

_____

_____

_____

_____

_____

_____

_____

_____

_____

_____

_____

_____

_____

_____

_____

_____

_____

_____

_____

_____

_____

_____

_____

_____

_____

November 16

HALF THE BATTLE IS OVER

"How skilled you are at pursuing love! Even the worst of women can learn from your ways."

—Jeremiah 2:33

You are not a failure. I say this with all my heart. *You are not a failure.* You've just been applying the wrong procedures to this choice of overindulging or this desire to end the strongholds in your life. You are not lazy ... in fact, you have been putting a great deal of effort and money into changing your environment (such as the content of food), but your attempts have not worked.

But this is very important—you have what it takes to be thin or to let go of any stronghold. To change, you must stop loving the world and start loving God. You may feel that you don't have love or that you don't know *how* to love God, but you do. The passage from Jeremiah refers to the love we have been giving to the world. You *already* have a heart of love, and that is half the battle! It is just that you have been giving your love to strongholds, not to God. God has seen that you are very skilled at pursuing your true love. For those who love food, He has seen you dream about food, dress for food, and care about the content, presentation, taste, and refrigeration of food. You have listened for the voice of food and responded when it called your name. You have encouraged others to appreciate food. Yes, you have been a good advocate for and obedient servant to your food god. So you see, you *are* a good lover. What a relief! Because love is the answer for being set free from strongholds of any kind! Now transfer that love to your patient, deserving heavenly Father!

November 17

How I Can Do God's Will Today

_____

_____

_____

_____

_____

_____

_____

_____

_____

_____

_____

_____

_____

_____

_____

_____

_____

_____

_____

_____

_____

_____

_____

_____

_____

_____

_____

_____

_____

_____

_____

_____

November 18

Put On the New

You, however, did not come to know Christ that way. Surely you heard of him and were taught in him in accordance with the truth that is in Jesus. You were taught, with regard to your former way of life, to put off your old self, which is being corrupted by its deceitful desires; to be made new in the attitude of your minds; and to put on the new self, created to be like God in true righteousness and holiness. Therefore each of you must put off falsehood and speak truthfully to his neighbor, for we are all members of one body. "In your anger do not sin": Do not let the sun go down while you are still angry, and do not give the devil a foothold. He who has been stealing must steal no longer, but must work, doing something useful with his own hands, that he may have something to share with those in need.

—Ephesians 4:20–28

Put to death your old habits. God tells us that we must rid ourselves of these things. He does not care how you kill the sinful desires of your old life ... *just do it*. Do not give your old temptations the time of day. Put out the fire of these desires any way you can. Put out the fire by throwing dust on it, making sure it has no oxygen. That way, you will put to death your old desires, and they will not tempt you anymore. You will have a new self, following God's desires for your life and your everyday activities! Notice from this passage that we are to really clean up our lives. The passage continues, "Be kind and compassionate to one another, forgiving each other, just as in Christ God forgave you. Be imitators of God, therefore, as dearly loved children and live a life of love, just as Christ loved us and gave himself up for us as a fragrant offering and sacrifice to God" (Ephesians 4:32–5:2).

November 11

How I Can Do God's Will Today

_____

_____

_____

_____

_____

_____

_____

_____

_____

_____

_____

_____

_____

_____

_____

_____

_____

_____

_____

_____

_____

_____

_____

_____

_____

_____

_____

_____

_____

November 20

GIVE GOD THE CREDIT HE DESERVES

But Moses said, "Here I am among six hundred thousand men on foot, and you say, 'I will give them meat to eat for a whole month!' Would they have enough if flocks and herds were slaughtered for them? Would they have enough if all the fish in the sea were caught for them?"

—Numbers 11:21–22

God told Moses to tell the people, "Get ready because I am going to provide meat for everyone tomorrow." Well, even Moses was shortsighted, and he questioned the Lord. We never give God the credit He deserves. Too few people see His resources, His power, His coordination, and His genius. God was begging, "Why don't you just trust in Me? Why don't you just trust in Me?" Read what God had to say to Moses in the next verse: "The LORD answered Moses, 'Is the LORD's arm too short? You will now see whether or not what I say will come true for you'" (Numbers 11:23).

God has accomplished beyond what I can think or imagine for my life. He will do the same for you as you continue to pursue righteousness and love. Trust Him!

November 27

HOW I CAN DO GOD'S WILL TODAY

_____

_____

_____

_____

_____

_____

_____

_____

_____

_____

_____

_____

_____

_____

_____

_____

_____

_____

_____

_____

_____

_____

_____

_____

_____

_____

_____

_____

_____

_____

_____

November 22

AUTHORITY ESTABLISHED BY GOD

Submit to one another out of reverence for Christ. Wives, submit to your husbands as to the Lord. For the husband is the head of the wife as Christ is the head of the church, his body, of which he is the Savior. Now as the church submits to Christ, so also wives should submit to their husbands in everything. Husbands, love your wives, just as Christ loved the church and gave himself up for her to make her holy, cleansing her by the washing with water through the word, and to present her to himself as a radiant church, without stain or wrinkle or any other blemish, but holy and blameless. In this same way, husbands ought to love their wives as their own bodies. He who loves his wife loves himself.

—*Ephesians 5:21–28*

Don't be afraid to submit to any authority that God has put before you on this earth. Remember, He places all people who are in authority, although we can't understand it sometimes or we know that the authority is less than perfect. When you submit to authority, postponing your control and relinquishing decisions to God, you are in essence believing in God's timing, waiting for God's permission, blessings, and approval to go ahead. You are proclaiming silently to the world that you believe God is great!

Submission to authority makes everything work smoothly. Have you ever seen people in the workplace who seemed perfectly content under submission—in fact, joyful and almost bubbling with life in that position? They have discovered that submission to authority connects them with the one in authority. The two now have a bridge to get to know each other, which results in becoming interwoven and united, and eventually the employee will be blessed and promoted by the one in authority. It is fun to watch God come back and give you what you want when you submit. You finally see that God speaks through earthly authority. Realizing this makes it easier and easier to submit until it becomes automatic to trust in God's plan.

November 23

HOW I CAN DO GOD'S WILL TODAY

November 24

SIN WILL MAKE YOUR BODY ACHE

Because of your wrath there is no health in my body; my bones have no soundness because of my sin. My guilt has overwhelmed me like a burden too heavy to bear. My wounds fester and are loathsome because of my sinful folly. I am bowed down and brought very low; all day long I go about mourning. My back is filled with searing pain; there is no health in my body. I am feeble and utterly crushed; I groan in anguish of heart. All my longings lie open before you, O Lord; my sighing is not hidden from you. My heart pounds, my strength fails me; even the light has gone from my eyes . . . For I am about to fall, and my pain is ever with me. I confess my iniquity; I am troubled by my sin.

—Psalm 38:3–10, 17–18

The physical feeling of guilt and depression is a sick feeling. It is real. You are not imagining it. We can see in these verses from the psalm that King David experienced guilt and depression in a physical way after his heart went astray. He knew that his sin caused his ailments, for he admitted, "My bones have no soundness because of my sin." King David was depressed, feeling guilty, and in pain because he knocked God off the throne and became the boss and made bad decisions. (We *are* bad gods.) In today's age of overly prescribed antidepressants, it is important to note that King David did not say that his feelings were the result of a physiological sickness, a chemical misfire, a genetic flaw, or a dysfunctional family. No, he admitted that the source of his sickness was his *own* sin. It was not from an illness to be covered up with medication. It was not from surrounding circumstances. It was from a heart that rebelled against God Almighty. We should examine our arrogant attitudes and realize that depression and ailments can come from kicking God off the throne of our hearts.

November 25

HOW I CAN DO GOD'S WILL TODAY

November 26

CHOOSE TODAY

*"Now fear the LORD and serve him with all faithfulness. Throw away
the gods your forefathers worshiped beyond the River and in Egypt, and
serve the LORD. But if serving the LORD seems undesirable to you, then
choose for yourselves this day whom you will serve, whether the gods
your forefathers served beyond the River, or the gods of the Amorites, in
whose land you are living. But as for me and my household, we will
serve the LORD."*

—Joshua 24:14–15

What happens if the heart is divided? If we love God, can we
love food too? Well, my friends, it is impossible. Matthew
told us in no uncertain terms that we cannot have two masters. You
cannot serve both God and food. Now, you were born to love, you
were born to worship, and you were born to serve. But you cannot
love, worship, and serve two things at one time. God ingeniously
programmed your heart to work in this way. You must *choose* today
which god you will serve—the things of the world or the one true
God Almighty—and then prove your choice by your deeds.

Practically all the authors of the Bible brought up this major pre-
cept of God. Jesus pointed out that there are two doors—one is wide
and leads to destruction, and one is narrow and leads to life. In the
passage from Joshua 24, Joshua made it clear that there are only two
choices—serving other gods or serving the Lord. Be aware, and don't
listen to Satan's lie that you can serve two masters. Instead, make
your choice to serve our awesome God through Jesus Christ.

November 27

How I Can Do God's Will Today

November 28

FIXING THE WORLD BY FIXING YOUR HEART

"Why do you look at the speck of sawdust in your brother's eye and pay no attention to the plank in your own eye? How can you say to your brother, 'Let me take the speck out of your eye,' when all the time there is a plank in your own eye? You hypocrite, first take the plank out of your own eye, and then you will see clearly to remove the speck from your brother's eye."

—Matthew 7:3–5

It is sometimes difficult to tell that the people who love to control are not on the right track. They may look the most righteous of all the sinners. After all, they devote their hearts and souls to cleaning up the "world." They pour hours of their time and lots of their energy into trying to change everything (and everyone) around them. After cleaning up the home environment and their families, they work on cleaning up the school and the teachers and curriculum, and then there are the church and the government . . . The process is never-ending, but it never leads to looking inward at themselves. After all, they are too busy looking at everyone else! I ask you today to let go of trying to fix anything outside yourself. Let God take care of all that. Instead, take all that energy and focus on scrubbing down your heart. It will take all the energy you have—plus the energy of God—to accomplish just that. Then God might lead you to help someone who is sinning, for you will be able to be merciful and you will be able to see more clearly!

November 21

How I Can Do God's Will Today

November 30

GRACE VERSUS WORKS

For of this you can be sure: No immoral, impure or greedy person—such a man is an idolater—has any inheritance in the kingdom of Christ and of God. Let no one deceive you with empty words, for because of such things God's wrath comes on those who are disobedient. Therefore do not be partners with them.   *—Ephesians 5:5–7*

But mark this: There will be terrible times in the last days. People will be lovers of themselves, lovers of money, boastful, proud, abusive, disobedient to their parents, ungrateful, unholy, without love, unforgiving, slanderous, without self-control, brutal, not lovers of the good, treacherous, rash, conceited, lovers of pleasure rather than lovers of God—having a form of godliness but denying its power. Have nothing to do with them.   *—2 Timothy 3:1–5*

The Bible is clear that you cannot do external work to enter the kingdom of God. You are saved by grace through Jesus Christ, whose sacrifice made it possible for you to be forgiven for kicking God off the throne of your heart and becoming arrogant, thinking you could rule your own life. The Cross gives us the opportunity to come back into God's kingdom under His rule. When you come into this sonship, crying out, "Abba, Father, Lord and Master, Rightful King," you become a new creation because God is ruling your heart now. The famous passage of "grace versus works" found in Ephesians 2:8 could not possibly be referring to *laying down sin* because the entire letter is largely about *turning from* sin: "...to put off your old self, which is being corrupted by its deceitful desires...and to put on the new self, created to be like God in true righteousness and holiness" (Ephesians 4:22–24). Grace is a gift from God, for Him to be Lord of our lives, and I am *thrilled* to have this opportunity. Bowing to His Lordship in every area of life is not a work—it's natural. The "work" noted by Paul means that you cannot follow legalistic rituals and offer "sorries" or sacrifices to get your way into heaven.

—December 7

How I Can Do God's Will Today

_____
_____
_____
_____
_____
_____
_____
_____
_____
_____
_____
_____
_____
_____
_____
_____
_____
_____
_____
_____
_____
_____
_____
_____
_____
_____
_____
_____
_____
_____
_____
_____

~December 2

EXCHANGING OUR GOD

"Therefore I bring charges against you again," declares the LORD. *"And I will bring charges against your children's children. Cross over to the coasts of Kittim and look, send to Kedar and observe closely; see if there has ever been anything like this: Has a nation ever changed its gods? (Yet they are not gods at all.) But my people have exchanged their Glory for worthless idols. Be appalled at this, O heavens, and shudder with great horror," declares the* LORD.

—Jeremiah 2:9–12

Have you realized what has happened to Christians around the world? The only group called to serve God the Father has casually exchanged Him for food and other idols or strongholds. This is not the first time such a thing has happened. Jeremiah told us that the Israelites exchanged God for worthless idols. So let's listen to this warning, a warning to the religious, to the churchgoers, to God's people—a warning to be careful not to surround ourselves with teachings that use the blood of Christ to allow us to exchange gods casually. Jesus' blood was never intended to leave us in Egypt, enslaved to false gods. Jesus was sent to set the captives free by forgiving us of our old loves and showing us the way to love the Father. We get to serve and follow the one true God because of Jesus Christ.

Many people have exchanged *the* Jesus Christ for a wimpy Jesus who would *never* say, "unless you repent, you too will all perish" (Luke 13:5), or "If your eye causes you to sin, pluck it out" (Mark 9:47a). The Apostle Paul said, "For if someone comes to you and preaches a Jesus other than the Jesus we preached, or if you receive a different spirit from the one you received, or a different gospel from the one you accepted, you put up with it easily enough" (2 Corinthians 11:4). I pray that we will not exchange our God and Jesus for another god. God has done nothing to deserve this!

—December 3

HOW I CAN DO GOD'S WILL TODAY

—December 4

No Middle Ground

Do not love the world or anything in the world. If anyone loves the world, the love of the Father is not in him.

— 1 John 2:15

Moses cried out in Deuteronomy 30 that there were only two choices, and he called them "life" and "death." Ezekiel pointed out that there were only two choices: righteousness and unrighteousness. The writer of Hebrews made sure that we understood that there were only two categories: the obedient and the disobedient, the believer and the unbeliever. The Apostle John wrote of only two types of people: those who love and those who hate. And God Himself gave us two choices in Exodus 20: hate Him or love Him. Never, in any of these categories, is there the slightest hint of an unattached or lukewarm option. There is no middle ground. All throughout the Old and New Testaments, God gets upset at His children for turning to another lover, much less trying to talk Him into letting all *three* into the same relationship. That is analogous to asking your spouse to allow you to have a second lover in bed with him! This is unthinkable, especially to such a wonderful God. Choose to turn to Him, and give Him your heart for good.

How I Can Do God's Will Today

December 6

TAPPING INTO GOD'S POWER

So I say, live by the Spirit, and you will not gratify the desires of the sinful nature. For the sinful nature desires what is contrary to the Spirit, and the Spirit what is contrary to the sinful nature . . . But the fruit of the Spirit is love, joy, peace, patience, kindness, goodness, faithfulness, gentleness and self-control. Against such things there is no law. Those who belong to Christ Jesus have crucified the sinful nature with its passions and desires.

—Galatians 5:16–17a, 22–24

Do you feel tired in the desert? Maybe you are using your own willpower. When you live according to your sinful nature, there is no way you can live the way God desires. These are opposite areas, and you cannot live both ways at once. Our Father wants us to live according to the Spirit, obeying His commands and loving Him above all else. Most of us want to please the Father, but we continually take over, day after day. Then we pray for forgiveness, try to repent, but again go back to telling God what to do.

The answer is to live by the Spirit, that is, do what God wants every day, all day long. When you submit, God can take control of your actions because He is on the throne of your heart, and His holy personality is love, joy, peace, patience, kindness, faithfulness, gentleness, goodness, and self-control.

—December 7

How I Can Do God's Will Today

_____

_____

_____

_____

_____

_____

_____

_____

_____

_____

_____

_____

_____

_____

_____

_____

_____

_____

_____

_____

_____

_____

_____

_____

_____

_____

_____

_____

_____

_____

_____

_____

— December 8

MOVING YOUR LIPS
AND NOT YOUR HEART

"...Isaiah was right when he prophesied about you hypocrites; as it is written: 'These people honor me with their lips, but their hearts are far from me.'"

—Mark 7:6

Have you ever heard of the expression "giving lip service"? That means that someone says just what should be said, but his true feelings are the opposite. He provides support with his lips by the words he says, but his heart is far away. Can you *verbally* give honor and glory to God, and yet your *heart* does not care at all? Of course you can. Your heart could be very far away from the Father right now, even as you read His Word and study His lessons. Search your heart, and make sure that you do not repeat history by honoring God only with your lips. Honor Him with your heart, and out of the abundance of the heart, the mouth will speak.

An easy way to understand how God feels about lip service is to imagine someone who acts as if he likes the boss. However, when the boss turns her back, he does what he wants at work. Then there are employees who do their work, but they have no devotion to the employer. If you get paid at McDonald's, why would you tell everyone the hamburgers are better at Burger King? No, even a child understands devotion to his parents. We must give God true devotion, shown through our lips, our hearts, *and* our actions.

—December 9

How I Can Do God's Will Today

—December 10

PERFECT LOVE CASTS OUT FEAR

There is no fear in love. But perfect love drives out fear, because fear has to do with punishment. The one who fears is not made perfect in love.

— 1 John 4:18

When you surrender your very life to the Father, you begin to know about His system of justice. You learn to believe in Him as the CEO of all business. You experience how He feeds you, protects you, defends you, and teaches you. You develop trust that He is there for your own good, that He sees your needs, and that He is going to take care of you, just as He has cared for every animal, every bird, every fish of the sea, every baby, every child, every woman and man, every race—*everyone.* When we don't know Him, we don't love or trust Him, and our lack of love makes us afraid that we will not be taken care of. But if you stay in the desert, you can reverse this process. You will learn to love and be loved, and perfect love casts out all fear.

When you are in the desert, you are hungry financially, relationally, and many other ways. These hungers—if you wait on the Lord—will be met by Him, and you will learn to love Him and trust Him. Without hard times, you would never call on Him and watch Him work them out. Make sure, however, you do not mess up this process by grabbing or taking care of self. Take care of God, and He will take care of you. Too cool!

— December 11

HOW I CAN DO GOD'S WILL TODAY

— December 12

LIVE BY THE SPIRIT

For if you live according to the sinful nature, you will die; but if by the Spirit you put to death the misdeeds of the body, you will live.

—Romans 8:13

The Spirit is not a vapor or mist. The Spirit of God and Christ is a loving heart and love from above. There is no other source of love. God's Spirit is a "good attitude" spirit. You need to develop the same focus and attitude of Christ. What was the mind-set or spirit of Christ? It was to please the Father and to do His will. Although just a part of the makeup of the "spirit" of Christ that is talked about in this passage, that attitude is still an important part. We are talking about the power that raised Christ Jesus from the dead. This submissive power will give life to our mortal bodies! Ask God to take away all the bad attitudes and hate within you, and ask Him for His great personality to fill your heart. He wants you to ask for it, He wants you to have it, and He wants you to live by it. This is the major key to unlocking your strongholds. Your decision to continue to overeat or indulge in anything that God has said "no" to comes directly from you—you are arrogant enough to think that you have the *right* to defy your Boss and that you deserve *more* than the indulgence that God generously has given you already. Change this ridiculous attitude—for you deserve nothing—and you will not overeat, overdrink, overtalk, or oversleep anymore! You are now living in step with God's Spirit or will, not your own.

—*December 13*

HOW I CAN DO GOD'S WILL TODAY

_____

_____

_____

_____

_____

_____

_____

_____

_____

_____

_____

_____

_____

_____

_____

_____

_____

_____

_____

_____

_____

_____

_____

_____

_____

_____

_____

_____

— December 14

He Sends Lightning with the Rain

This is what the LORD says: "See, I will stir up the spirit of a destroyer against Babylon and the people of Leb Kamai. I will send foreigners to Babylon to winnow her and to devastate her land."

—Jeremiah 51:1–2a

"When he thunders, the waters in the heavens roar; he makes clouds rise from the ends of the earth. He sends lightning with the rain and brings out the wind from his storehouses."

—Jeremiah 51:16

"I will bring them down like lambs to the slaughter, like rams and goats."

—Jeremiah 51:40

When will we learn that God is highly involved, from storms and disasters to the best of blessings? After King Nebuchadnezzar lived as an animal in the wild for seven years, he lifted his eyes toward heaven and praised God, saying, "All the peoples of the earth are regarded as nothing. He does as he pleases with the powers of heaven and the peoples of the earth. No one can hold back his hand or say to him: 'What have you done?'" (Daniel 4:35).

God is God, and I love it! I don't want it any other way, and I wouldn't want the world in the hands of anyone else. God has all authority and power, and I respect and uphold every decision He makes—even the difficult ones. No one should call himself a disciple of Christ until he contemplates that God caused His only Son to suffer (Isaiah 53:10). And then that God has called us to walk in Jesus' steps. The good news is that Jesus was rewarded and is at the right-hand side of the God of the universe.

—December 15

HOW I CAN DO GOD'S WILL TODAY

—December 16

DRY BONES

Then he said to me, "Prophesy to these bones and say to them, 'Dry bones, hear the word of the LORD! This is what the Sovereign LORD says to these bones: I will make breath enter you, and you will come to life. I will attach tendons to you and make flesh come upon you and cover you with skin; I will put breath in you, and you will come to life. Then you will know that I am the LORD.'" . . . Then he said to me: "Son of man, these bones are the whole house of Israel. They say, 'Our bones are dried up and our hope is gone; we are cut off.' Therefore prophesy and say to them: 'This is what the Sovereign LORD says: O my people, I am going to open your graves and bring you up from them; I will bring you back to the land of Israel. Then you, my people, will know that I am the LORD, when I open your graves and bring you up from them. I will put my Spirit in you and you will live, and I will settle you in your own land. Then you will know that I the LORD have spoken, and I have done it, declares the LORD.'"

—Ezekiel 37:4–6, 11–14

If your life seems dry in your desert journey and you don't have any "get up and go" in your bones, then you might need to call out to the Lord for help. You are nothing without Him, just dry bones with no life. God can put life back in your bones and put His great personality and Spirit back in your heart. This concept is absolutely crucial to life. If you want to do things His way, then you are the *called out*—the army God is looking for. He cannot live in you until you are dry bones—in other words, until your will has died. There is no spirit like the Spirit of God. May we all allow Him to come and completely rule His people!

—December 17

HOW I CAN DO GOD'S WILL TODAY

_____

_____

_____

_____

_____

_____

_____

_____

_____

_____

_____

_____

_____

_____

_____

_____

_____

_____

_____

_____

_____

_____

_____

_____

_____

_____

_____

_____

—December 18

THE PRIDE OF LIFE

Praise be to the LORD, for he showed his wonderful love to me when I was in a besieged city. In my alarm I said, "I am cut off from your sight!" Yet you heard my cry for mercy when I called to you for help. Love the LORD, all his saints! The LORD preserves the faithful, but the proud he pays back in full. Be strong and take heart, all you who hope in the LORD.

—Psalm 31:21–24

When you are feeling low, remember that the Lord preserves the faithful—those who believe that God is a worthy Boss who deserves our undivided devotion. God opposes the proud and pays them back in full for thinking that they are smarter than He is or thinking that they deserve more than what God has provided for indulgence. The lust of the flesh, the lust of the eyes, and the pride of life all boil down to sin (1 John 2:16). All of it says you want even *more*. You are actually greedy for more than what God has generously given. If you are not happy on earth with the amount that God has allotted, you will complain in heaven, too. Get rid of pride. God made *you* to obey—not vice versa! Praise God that there will be no greed in heaven!

For of this you can be sure: No immoral, impure or greedy person— such a man is an idolater—has any inheritance in the kingdom of Christ and of God.

—Ephesians 5:5

—December 11

HOW I CAN DO GOD'S WILL TODAY

— December 20

THROUGH THE NARROW DOOR

Then Jesus went through the towns and villages, teaching as he made his way to Jerusalem. Someone asked him, "Lord, are only a few people going to be saved?" He said to them, "Make every effort to enter through the narrow door, because many, I tell you, will try to enter and will not be able to. Once the owner of the house gets up and closes the door, you will stand outside knocking and pleading, 'Sir, open the door for us.' But he will answer, 'I don't know you or where you come from.' Then you will say, 'We ate and drank with you, and you taught in our streets.' But he will reply, 'I don't know you or where you come from. Away from me, all you evildoers!'"

—Luke 13:22–27

Don't be bothered or tempted today because everyone you know rejects the freedom you now have with food. When a person's heart is out of control, it cannot comprehend the freedom that another person could have with regular foods. More than likely you will always be in the minority, but that does not make you wrong. It sometimes means you are exactly on target! Even though we might be eager to share this way of life with everyone we know, not everyone will understand it. As Jesus stated, "narrow [is] the road that leads to life, and only a few find it" (Matthew 7:14). We need to seek out what our God wants and obey it. Many people *guessed* at what they thought God wanted, but they never really *submitted* to His leadership; instead, they were self-employed or employed by Satan. Therefore, on Judgment Day, God and Jesus will not recognize them because God never employed them. Stay in God's Word, and look intently into His will.

—December 21

HOW I CAN DO GOD'S WILL TODAY

_____

_____

_____

_____

_____

_____

_____

_____

_____

_____

_____

_____

_____

_____

_____

_____

_____

_____

_____

_____

_____

_____

_____

_____

_____

_____

_____

_____

_____

_____

_____

_____

 —December 22

ARE YOU WORTHY?

"Anyone who loves his father or mother more than me is not worthy of me; anyone who loves his son or daughter more than me is not worthy of me; and anyone who does not take his cross and follow me is not worthy of me."

—Matthew 10:37–38

People wrongly say, "I am not worthy of God," because they do not feel good about themselves. Well, Jesus said that you are *precious*. You are *not* worthy if you love something else above Him. You are arrogant at this stage since you don't believe you need to bow down to God's will. You might feel above God, but you are not feeling unworthy. Don't get confused.

Now remember, after God tests you with food, He will test you with your family and friends. You must be strong and ready for that test because God becomes jealous if you love your family members more than you love Him. Making Him first in your life means first above everything, not just first over food or other false idols. Just as we should not make food into a god, we cannot make a spouse or child into a god. Food has a purpose in our lives, and so do our family members. Pray that God will guide your family according to His will, and pray that He will lead the heart of each family member. And always remember that whatever you give to God, He will give back. In Mark 10:29–30, Jesus said that no one who has left home or brothers or sisters or mother or father or children or fields for Him and the gospel will fail to receive a hundred times as much in this present age, and in the age to come will receive eternal life. We need never worry about anything if we remember to keep God first above all else. The hearts that love are worthy, and they are wonderful to the Father!

—December 23

How I Can Do God's Will Today

~December 24

LOWER YOURSELF AND
YOU WILL BE LIFTED UP

If you have any encouragement from being united with Christ, if any comfort from his love, if any fellowship with the Spirit, if any tenderness and compassion, then make my joy complete by being like-minded, having the same love, being one in spirit and purpose. Do nothing out of selfish ambition or vain conceit, but in humility consider others better than yourselves. Each of you should look not only to your own interests, but also to the interests of others. Your attitude should be the same as that of Christ Jesus: Who, being in very nature God, did not consider equality with God something to be grasped, but made himself nothing, taking the very nature of a servant, being made in human likeness. And being found in appearance as a man, he humbled himself and became obedient to death—even death on a cross! Therefore God exalted him to the highest place and gave him the name that is above every name, that at the name of Jesus every knee should bow, in heaven and on earth and under the earth, and every tongue confess that Jesus Christ is Lord, to the glory of God the Father.

—Philippians 2:1–11

The world will tell you that you deserve something great. Taking care of "#1" will be the most logical temptation in life. You will be tempted to remove yourself from the altar, and emptying yourself will not be natural. But if you give in to the temptation, you will miss the incredible work of the Mighty Warrior and Savior. If you let your Hero, God Almighty, save you, you will have peace and joy and will receive honor from those around you. Jesus did not give in to the temptation to save Himself from the cross, and He is now sitting on the right-hand side of God. He set out to obey God and face the death He was called to. Luke 9:51 says, "As the time approached for him to be taken up to heaven, Jesus resolutely set out for Jerusalem." You must resolutely set out to obey God as well. Jesus rose from the *dead*. Do not be afraid of death to yourself, for you will rise!

—December 25

HOW I CAN DO GOD'S WILL TODAY

_____
_____
_____
_____
_____
_____
_____
_____
_____
_____
_____
_____
_____
_____
_____
_____
_____
_____
_____
_____
_____
_____
_____
_____
_____
_____
_____
_____
_____
_____

~December 26

You Have No One to Fear

The LORD is my light and my salvation—whom shall I fear? The LORD is the stronghold of my life—of whom shall I be afraid? When evil men advance against me to devour my flesh, when my enemies and my foes attack me, they will stumble and fall. Though an army besiege me, my heart will not fear; though war break out against me, even then will I be confident.

—Psalm 27:1–3

We must remember not to panic when Satan is attacking or falsely accusing the servants of the Lord. After all, if God is the stronghold of your life, you have no one to fear. God will defend you, strengthen you, and guide you. Satan will try everything he can to bring your attitude down, to make you doubt yourself and God, and to thwart any good work you are doing for God's kingdom. Sometimes I think I see a little smoke from Satan, and I prepare for trouble. But when I examine it closely, God shows me that there is no fire. Every time I think I see an attack coming, I get on my knees and pray for protection. I rise to my feet, confident of the Lord's power, and by the next day or so the threat of the enemy is over. God puts out all the fires of Satan!

The main thing to do is to turn to the Word of God where you will see all of God's people threatened (especially with slander), but the answer is to make sure that you keep focused on *knowing, loving,* and *obeying* God's Word. Please stay in the Word, and have a great attitude of trust and joy in God. Then when you are threatened, you can sing in the prison as Paul did. The next thing you know—the angels will open the prison doors (Acts 5:19).

—*December 27*

How I Can Do God's Will Today

_____
_____
_____
_____
_____
_____
_____
_____
_____
_____
_____
_____
_____
_____
_____
_____
_____
_____
_____
_____
_____
_____
_____
_____
_____
_____
_____
_____
_____
_____
_____

―December 28

COUNT YOUR BLESSINGS

At that time the disciples came to Jesus and asked, "Who is the greatest in the kingdom of heaven?" He called a little child and had him stand among them. And he said: "I tell you the truth, unless you change and become like little children, you will never enter the kingdom of heaven. Therefore, whoever humbles himself like this child is the greatest in the kingdom of heaven."

—Matthew 18:1–4

Jesus and the prophets were trying to make things very clear for the people by using parables and stories that portrayed the will of God as revealed in the scriptures. The only scriptures that they had available were in the Old Testament, and what God wanted and was going to fulfill in Christ is very clear in the Psalms, Isaiah, and the Minor Prophets. But instead of creating His sermons by quoting Isaiah or David, Jesus told the same message of repentance in a fresh way—you cannot stay the same. Here, Jesus said you must be like children to enter the kingdom. Jesus was looking for *humility*. Having humility does not mean staying in the background or being shy. Think about a young child: he makes his presence known, yet he wakes up happy, holding no grudges, and he does not expect anything but takes the food and the agenda offered for the day. He is happy—no, *thrilled*—with little surprises, and he is fascinated with creation. With no pride, he gives thanks to God at night. He loves the parent and does not correct that authority as if he had a better idea. He falls to sleep and dreams of playing and happy thoughts with no expectation or demands on what the morrow will bring. We cannot enter God's business or kingdom if we do not humble ourselves and get a good attitude. We must not complain or have certain expectations; rather, we must be thankful and full of praise for this great Father and King! I love this genius plan of God's!

—December 21

How I Can Do God's Will Today

_____

_____

_____

_____

_____

_____

_____

_____

_____

_____

_____

_____

_____

_____

_____

_____

_____

_____

_____

_____

_____

_____

_____

_____

_____

_____

_____

_____

_____

—December 30

THE PROMISE OF ENTERING

Therefore, since the promise of entering his rest still stands, let us be careful that none of you be found to have fallen short of it.

—Hebrews 4:1

The grace of God can be summed up as a proposal from God to us because He wants to be the object of our affection. It is like being invited to join a company with which you have been seeking employment for a long time. It is a wonderful opportunity to have a new boss! If you have ever had a terrible employer and then got a new job under a very loving employer, it is a rush of emotion for you! The Israelites loved leaving the oppression of slavery. God has given us the promise of a wonderful, new job—we will be employed as His devoted followers and defenders, and the rewards will be great!

The prodigal son finally came to his senses and saw the grace of God. He saw that being invited to be a mere slave in the house of God was an incredible opportunity, not to mention being invited back as a true child of God. Do not snub the grace of God and this awesome proposal from Him. I am thrilled to be called as a soldier, a daughter, a bride, an employee, a servant, a friend. It is really hard to believe that I am living and have an opportunity to "apply" to this great heavenly empire. The promise of entering still stands; let us be careful that none of us are found to have fallen short.

—December 31

INDEX OF READINGS

ENCOURAGING MATERIALS

Weigh Down at Home is the indispensable tool for all Weigh Down participants. Twelve video lessons are presented in a warm and inviting environment. Audiotapes reinforce the message—convenient for car or home use. Inspiring and encouraging booklets share tons of scripture and timely tips as you go through your week. The workbook ties the whole program together. *Weigh Down at Home* is just what you need to move you beyond your struggles, or to help reinforce the message of death to self that is taught in all of the seminar series.

Have you struggled with weight loss issues most of your life? Are you tired of going from one failed diet to the next? *Rise Above* is the answer you've been seeking, and it's not even a diet—it's a whole new way of living for God! This follow-up to the best-selling *Weigh Down Diet* book can help take away your desire to overeat. Others may help change your habits, but *Rise Above* will touch your heart, soul, mind, and spirit. It will transform you into a new person!

The basics of the Weigh Down Workshop seminar in book form, *The Weigh Down Diet* is a great companion guide for Weigh Down seminar participants. Find out why over one million copies of this book have been sold!

Foxe's Book of Martyrs chronicles men and women in the fourteenth through sixteenth centuries who valued the truth about God above their own short life. This exciting new publication goes hand in hand with the message of the *Weigh Down Advanced* seminar series about complete death to self and totally living for God! Pick it up now, and prepare to be inspired by the great cloud of witnesses as you seek to **DO** God's will.

Check for frequent updates, sign up for the email list, participate in encouraging forums, and more at:

www.wdworkshop.com

ENCOURAGING SEMINARS

Weigh Down Advanced is the newest seminar from the Weigh Down Workshop, specially designed for the individual who has been through *EXODUS Out of Egypt*, *EXODUS from Strongholds*, and/or *Weigh Down at Home*. This series is a firm, yet loving, call to participants to finally give up the desire for control and crown God through their obedience.

Testimonies are already coming in of past participants finally getting it, losing weight, and meeting with groups of like-minded Christians. The series includes:

‡   10 weeks of video seminar (videos are longer than 1 hour)

‡   Vinyl binder to hold workbook and audiotapes

‡   In-depth Bible study contained in the 168 page workbook

‡   10 audiotapes to reinforce the videos throughout your week

‡   Key and Truth Cards with a pouch to remind you that you are not your own and that you **can** lay down the sin in your life!

EXODUS Out of Egypt and *EXODUS from Strongholds* seminars are available in your area!

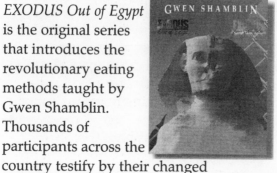

EXODUS Out of Egypt is the original series that introduces the revolutionary eating methods taught by Gwen Shamblin. Thousands of participants across the country testify by their changed lives!

EXODUS from Strongholds is the highly successful follow-up to the *Out of Egypt* seminar that shows participants how to overcome other areas of sin in their lives.

To find a pure fellowship of like-minded believers in your area, or more information on **Remnant Fellowships** go to:

www.remnantfellowship.org